EDGARDO FERNANDEZ CLIMENT

ITIL4 in Action:

A Step-by-Step Guide for IT Professionals

First edition

This book was professionally typeset on Reedsy.
Find out more at reedsy.com

For Graciela, my love,
This book is a tribute to the incredible woman who has been my pillar of
strength and the beating heart of our shared story.
With deep gratitude and all the love in my heart, I dedicate this work to you.
Edgardo

Contents

Chapter 1: Introduction to ITIL4

Understanding ITIL4 framework

In today's fast-paced and technology-driven world, IT professionals face numerous challenges when it comes to managing and delivering IT services effectively. To address these challenges, the IT Infrastructure Library (ITIL) framework has become a widely adopted and globally recognized approach. ITIL4, the latest iteration of this framework, offers a comprehensive and flexible set of guidelines for implementing best practices in IT service management.

This book aims to provide IT professionals with a step-by-step guide on how to implement ITIL4 in their organizations. By gaining a deeper understanding of the ITIL4 framework, IT professionals can enhance their ability to deliver high-quality IT services that align with their organization's objectives.

The ITIL4 framework focuses on creating value through the integration of IT services with business needs. It introduces several key concepts, including the **Service Value System (SVS)**, the **Four Dimensions of Service Management**, and the **Service Value Chain**. These concepts provide a holistic approach to managing IT services, enabling organizations to deliver value to their customers and stakeholders effectively.

The **SVS** forms the core of the ITIL4 framework, emphasizing the importance of collaboration and integration among various components of an organization. IT professionals will learn how to define their organization's vision, create a culture of continuous improvement, and establish effective governance and management practices.

The **Four Dimensions of Service Management** provide a comprehensive view of the different aspects that need to be considered when delivering IT services. These dimensions include organizations and people, information and technology, partners and suppliers, and value streams and processes. IT professionals will gain insights into how these dimensions interact and impact service delivery, helping them identify areas for improvement and implement effective strategies.

The **Service Value Chain** outlines the activities that organizations need to perform to deliver value to their customers. IT professionals will understand how to plan, engage, design, deliver, and support IT services, ensuring a seamless and efficient service delivery process.

By implementing ITIL4 in their organizations, IT professionals can improve service quality, enhance customer satisfaction, and increase operational efficiency. They will gain the knowledge and skills necessary to align IT services with business objectives, optimize resource utilization, and mitigate risks effectively.

By embracing the ITIL4 framework, IT professionals can enhance their ability to deliver high-quality IT services that align with their organization's goals.

IT Service Management (ITSM)

ITIL 4, or Information Technology Infrastructure Library version 4, is a framework for IT service management (ITSM) that provides a set of best practices for organizations to align their IT services with the needs of the business. ITIL 4 builds upon the previous versions of ITIL and is designed to address the challenges and opportunities presented by modern technology and business practices. ITSM, in the context of ITIL 4, refers to the strategies, processes, people, and technology used to deliver and manage IT services.

Here are key aspects of ITIL 4 ITSM:

1. Service Value System (SVS): ITIL 4 introduces the Service Value System, which is a holistic approach to service management. The SVS integrates various components, including the Service Value Chain, guiding principles, governance, and continual improvement, to create value for both the service provider and the customers.

2. Service Value Chain (SVC): The Service Value Chain is a set of interconnected activities that organizations perform to deliver a valuable product or service. The activities within the Service Value Chain include Plan, Improve, Engage, Design & Transition, Obtain/Build, and Deliver & Support.

3. Guiding Principles: ITIL 4 introduces seven guiding principles that guide organizations in their decision-making and actions. These principles include:
  - Focus on Value
  - Start Where You Are

- Progress Iteratively with Feedback
- Collaborate and Promote Visibility
- Think and Work Holistically
- Keep It Simple and Practical
- Optimize and Automate

4. Four Dimensions of Service Management:
- Organizations and People
- Information and Technology
- Value Streams and Processes
- Partners and Suppliers

These dimensions provide a comprehensive view of the factors that influence the design, development, and delivery of services.

5. ITIL Practices: ITIL 4 introduces a set of practices that cover a wide range of ITSM activities. Some of the key practices include:
- Incident Management
- Problem Management
- Change Control
- Service Level Management
- Continual Improvement
- Service Desk
- Service Request Management
- Release Management

6. Continual Improvement: ITIL 4 emphasizes the importance of continual improvement at all levels of the organization. This involves regularly assessing current practices, identifying areas for improvement, and implementing changes to enhance service delivery.

7. Governance: Governance in ITIL 4 refers to the establishment of policies, guidelines, and decision-making processes to ensure that the organization's resources are used effectively and aligned with its objectives.

ITIL 4 is designed to be more flexible and adaptable, allowing organizations to tailor their ITSM practices to their specific needs. It promotes a collaborative and value-driven approach to service management, focusing on delivering high-quality services that meet the changing demands of the business and its stakeholders.

Service Value System (SVS)

The ITIL 4 Service Value System (SVS) is a key framework introduced in ITIL 4, the latest version of the Information Technology Infrastructure Library (ITIL). The SVS is designed to provide a holistic approach to service management, integrating various components to create value for both the service provider and its customers. The SVS is centered around the concept of creating value through the co-creation of services.

Here are the main components of the ITIL 4 Service Value System:

1. **Service Value Chain (SVC):** The Service Value Chain is a set of interconnected activities that an organization performs to deliver a valuable product or service. It consists of six core activities:
   - Plan: Strategize and plan service delivery.
   - Improve: Continuously improve services, processes, and performance.
   - Engage: Engage with stakeholders and understand their needs.

- Design & Transition: Design, build, and transition new services.
- Obtain/Build: Obtain or build the necessary resources for service delivery.
- Deliver & Support: Deliver and support services to meet customer needs.

2. Guiding Principles: A set of fundamental principles that guide an organization in the decision-making process and behavior. Some of these principles include:
- Focus on Value
- Start Where You Are
- Progress Iteratively with Feedback
- Collaborate and Promote Visibility
- Think and Work Holistically

3. Governance: Governance refers to the establishment of policies and guidelines to ensure that the organization's resources are used effectively and aligned with its objectives. It involves making decisions, setting direction, and monitoring performance.

4. Service Value System Components:
- Service Value Chain: Described earlier, it represents the key activities required to create value.
- Inputs and Outputs: Resources, inputs, and outputs for each activity within the Service Value Chain.
- Practices: Sets of organizational resources and capabilities for performing work or accomplishing an objective. Examples include Incident Management, Problem Management, and Change Control.

5. Continual Improvement: The SVS emphasizes the importance of ongoing improvement in all aspects of service management. The organization is encouraged to regularly review its practices, services, and performance to identify opportunities for enhancement.

6. Service Value Streams: These represent the end-to-end activities required to deliver a product or service to a consumer. Each service value stream is associated with one or more service value chains.

7. External Factors: Consideration of external factors that may impact the organization's ability to deliver value, such as market trends, technology advancements, regulatory changes, and societal factors.

The ITIL 4 Service Value System provides a comprehensive and flexible framework for organizations to adopt a service-oriented approach, ensuring the creation and delivery of value to both the service provider and its customers.

Service Value Chain

The ITIL 4 Service Value Chain (SVC) is a core component of the ITIL 4 framework, introduced to guide organizations in creating, delivering, and continually improving services. The Service Value Chain is a set of interconnected activities that work together to produce value for both the service provider and the service consumer. It emphasizes a flexible and adaptive approach to service management, allowing organizations to tailor their practices to meet specific business needs. The Service Value Chain consists of six key activities:

1. Plan:
  - Objective: To ensure a shared understanding of the vision, current

status, and improvement opportunities.

- Key Activities: Establishing a strategy, defining objectives, identifying constraints, and planning for risk.

2. Improve:

- Objective: To continually align the organization's products and services with changing business needs.

- Key Activities: Identifying improvement opportunities, analyzing data, implementing changes, and measuring results.

3. Engage:

- Objective: To engage with stakeholders and understand their needs, expectations, and the context of service delivery.

- Key Activities: Establishing relationships with stakeholders, capturing and managing requirements, and ensuring effective communication.

4. Design & Transition:

- Objective: To design and transition new or changed services into operations.

- Key Activities: Designing services, developing service solutions, transitioning services, and validating changes.

5. Obtain/Build:

- Objective: To ensure that the organization has the resources needed to deliver services.

- Key Activities: Identifying, assessing, and acquiring resources; developing and managing partnerships; and ensuring resource availability.

6. Deliver & Support:

- Objective: To deliver services in accordance with agreed-upon service levels.

  - Key Activities: Managing service requests, resolving incidents and problems, ensuring access and availability, and fulfilling service requests.

The Service Value Chain is dynamic and iterative, allowing organizations to adapt to changes in technology, business requirements, and customer expectations. Each of the activities within the chain interacts with the others, and they can be performed in any order depending on the specific context and objectives of the organization. The goal is to create a flexible and efficient system for delivering value, with a focus on customer satisfaction and continual improvement.

It's important to note that the Service Value Chain is closely tied to the ITIL 4 guiding principles, which include principles such as "Focus on Value," "Start Where You Are," "Progress Iteratively with Feedback," "Collaborate and Promote Visibility," and "Think and Work Holistically." These principles provide additional guidance on how to effectively implement the activities within the Service Value Chain.

Guiding Principles

The ITIL 4 Guiding Principles are a set of seven fundamental recommendations that guide organizations in making decisions and adopting good practices for IT service management (ITSM). These principles are designed to be applicable across various contexts and provide a foundation for organizations to navigate the complexities of service management effectively. The guiding principles are:

1. Focus on Value:

- Principle: Organizations should focus on delivering value to their customers and stakeholders. Value is the central driving force, and all decisions and actions should align with creating, delivering, and maintaining value throughout the service lifecycle.

2. Start Where You Are:

- Principle: Organizations should acknowledge their current position and build upon existing assets and capabilities. Rather than starting from scratch, they should leverage existing processes, technologies, and resources to facilitate a more gradual and manageable improvement journey.

3. Progress Iteratively with Feedback:

- Principle: Iterative progress allows for incremental improvements. Organizations should continuously evaluate their practices, processes, and services. Feedback loops, both internal and external, play a crucial role in identifying areas for improvement and making necessary adjustments.

4. Collaborate and Promote Visibility:

- Principle: Collaboration is essential for effective service management. Organizations should foster a collaborative culture within and between teams, breaking down silos. Promoting visibility ensures that relevant information is shared transparently, contributing to better decision-making and understanding.

5. Think and Work Holistically:

- Principle: Organizations should consider the entire service value system rather than focusing solely on individual components or processes. A holistic perspective encourages a comprehensive understanding of how different parts of the organization interact and contribute to the delivery of value.

6. Keep It Simple and Practical:
  - Principle: Simplicity is a key consideration in service management. Organizations should avoid unnecessary complexity and prioritize simplicity and practicality in their processes, services, and technologies. This principle aligns with the idea that simpler solutions are often more sustainable and easier to maintain.

7. Optimize and Automate:
  - Principle: Continuous improvement is essential. Organizations should seek opportunities to optimize processes, reduce inefficiencies, and automate repetitive tasks where possible. Automation can enhance efficiency, accuracy, and consistency in service delivery.

These guiding principles are intended to be flexible and adaptable to different organizational contexts. By following these principles, organizations can make informed decisions, promote a culture of continuous improvement, and ensure that their ITSM practices align with business goals and deliver maximum value to customers and stakeholders. The guiding principles are an integral part of the ITIL 4 framework and complement the other components of ITIL, such as the Service Value System and the Four Dimensions of Service Management.

Four Dimensions of Service Management

The ITIL 4 Four Dimensions of Service Management is a framework that provides a comprehensive view of the various aspects that need to be considered for effective and holistic service management. These dimensions are critical to understanding the different perspectives and influences that impact the design, development, and delivery of services. The four dimensions are as follows:

1. Organizations and People:

- Organizational Structure: Examines the structure of the organization, including roles, responsibilities, and relationships, to ensure that it supports the effective delivery of services.

- Culture and Collaboration: Focuses on the culture within the organization, emphasizing the importance of a positive and collaborative environment for successful service management.

- Skills and Competencies: Addresses the skills and competencies required by individuals within the organization to perform their roles effectively and contribute to the delivery of high-quality services.

2. Information and Technology:

- Information: Refers to the data, knowledge, and information that are necessary for service management. It involves managing and leveraging information to support decision-making and service delivery.

- Technology: Encompasses the hardware, software, and other tools that support service management activities. It includes considerations for automation, monitoring, and other technological aspects that contribute to service delivery.

3. Value Streams and Processes:

- Value Streams: Describes the series of steps an organization uses to create and deliver value to its customers. Understanding and optimizing these value streams is crucial for efficient service delivery.

- Processes: Refers to the set of interrelated or interacting activities that transform inputs into outputs. ITIL 4 emphasizes the importance of flexible and agile processes that contribute to the overall value creation.

4. Partners and Suppliers:

- External Service Providers: Includes external entities that contribute to the delivery of services, such as suppliers, vendors, and partners. Managing these relationships effectively is essential for ensuring seamless service delivery.

- Service Value Network: Represents the complex web of interactions and dependencies between the organization and its partners and suppliers. This dimension emphasizes the need for collaboration and integration.

These four dimensions work together to provide a holistic view of service management. Effective service management requires considering each dimension and balancing their interdependencies. The Four Dimensions of Service Management in ITIL 4 help organizations address the complexity of the modern service environment and adapt to changing circumstances, ensuring that services are delivered with value and quality.

Practices

In ITIL 4, practices refer to sets of organizational resources and capabilities for performing work or achieving objectives. ITIL 4 introduces a comprehensive set of practices that cover a wide range of IT service management (ITSM) activities. These practices provide guidance on how to approach various aspects of service management, and they can be tailored to the specific needs and circumstances of an organization.

Here are some key ITIL 4 practices:

1. General Management Practices:

- Architecture Management: Provides guidance on designing and managing the organization's architecture to support its objectives.
- Continual Improvement: Focuses on regularly assessing services, processes, and practices to identify opportunities for improvement and drive ongoing enhancement.

2. Service Management Practices:

- Service Desk: Offers guidance on providing a single point of contact for users to report issues, request services, or seek assistance.
- Incident Management: Helps in restoring normal service operation as quickly as possible after an incident to minimize impact on business operations.
- Problem Management: Aims to prevent incidents from recurring by identifying and addressing the underlying causes of problems.
- Change Control: Provides guidance on managing changes to IT services in a controlled and efficient manner to minimize risk and disruption.

3. Technical Management Practices:

- Release Management: Ensures the planning, testing, and deployment of new or modified services, including hardware, software, processes, and documentation.
- Deployment Management: Focuses on deploying and implementing new or changed hardware, software, processes, and documentation into the live environment.

4. IT Asset Management Practices:

- Monitoring and Event Management: Involves monitoring the

infrastructure and IT services to detect and respond to events and alerts proactively.

- IT Asset Management: Helps in tracking and managing the organization's assets throughout their lifecycle.

5. Workforce and Talent Management Practices:

- Training and Awareness: Ensures that the workforce has the necessary skills and knowledge to perform their roles effectively.

- Workforce and Talent Management: Addresses the recruitment, development, and retention of skilled individuals to support IT service delivery.

6. Risk Management Practices:

- Risk Management: Identifies, assesses, and manages risks to minimize their impact on IT services and the organization.

7. Knowledge Management Practices:

- Knowledge Management: Involves capturing, organizing, storing, and sharing knowledge and information within the organization to support decision-making and service delivery.

8. Service Automation Practices:

- Infrastructure and Platform Management: Addresses the management and optimization of infrastructure and platforms to support service delivery.

- Software Development and Management: Focuses on managing the development and maintenance of software to support IT services.

These ITIL 4 practices are designed to be flexible and adaptable. Organizations can choose and combine practices based on their specific needs, considering factors such as the size of the organization, the complexity of services, and the nature of the industry. The goal is to create a tailored approach to ITSM that aligns with business objectives and delivers value to customers.

Benefits of implementing ITIL4 in your organization

This section explores the numerous benefits that IT professionals can gain by implementing ITIL4 in their organizations.

1. Improved Service Delivery: One of the key advantages of ITIL4 is its focus on customer-centric service delivery. By following ITIL4 principles and best practices, IT professionals can ensure that their services are aligned with the needs and expectations of their customers, resulting in improved customer satisfaction and loyalty.

2. Increased Efficiency and Effectiveness: ITIL4 offers a systematic approach to managing IT services, enabling organizations to streamline their processes and workflows. Through process standardization and automation, IT professionals can eliminate redundancies, reduce response times, and enhance productivity, resulting in increased efficiency and effectiveness.

3. Enhanced Risk Management: ITIL4 emphasizes the importance of risk management in IT service delivery. By adopting ITIL4's risk management practices, IT professionals can identify and mitigate potential risks, ensuring the continuity of critical IT services and minimizing the impact of incidents on business operations.

4. Better Decision-Making: ITIL4 provides a holistic view of IT service management, enabling IT professionals to make informed decisions based on reliable data and insights. With access to key performance indicators and metrics, organizations can monitor service performance, identify areas for improvement, and make data-driven decisions to enhance service quality and efficiency.

5. Cultivating a Culture of Continuous Improvement: ITIL4 promotes a culture of continuous improvement by encouraging organizations to regularly assess and refine their IT service management practices. By implementing ITIL4, IT professionals can establish a framework for continuous service improvement, fostering a culture of learning, innovation, and adaptability within the organization.

6. Increased Collaboration and Communication: ITIL4 emphasizes the importance of collaboration and communication between different IT teams and stakeholders. By implementing ITIL4 practices, IT professionals can break down silos, improve cross-functional collaboration, and enhance communication channels, resulting in better coordination, alignment, and synergy across the organization.

In conclusion, implementing ITIL4 in your organization offers numerous benefits for IT professionals. From improved service delivery and increased efficiency to enhanced risk management and better decision-making, ITIL4 provides a comprehensive framework that enables organizations to align their IT services with their business objectives. By adopting ITIL4's best practices, IT professionals can drive continuous improvement, foster collaboration, and ensure the delivery of high-quality IT services that meet the needs and expectations of their customers.

Chapter 2: Getting Started with ITIL4

Assessing your organization's current IT service management practices

In today's rapidly evolving digital landscape, effective IT service management is vital for organizations to maintain a competitive edge. As an IT professional, it is crucial to assess your organization's current IT service management practices to identify areas of improvement and implement ITIL4 – the latest version of the Information Technology Infrastructure Library – to enhance service delivery and align IT with business objectives.

Assessing the current state of IT service management practices provides valuable insights into existing strengths, weaknesses, and opportunities for improvement. It allows IT professionals to identify gaps in processes, technology, and skills that may hinder efficient service delivery. By conducting a thorough assessment, you can determine the areas where ITIL4 implementation will have the most significant impact and design a roadmap for successful adoption.

The assessment should encompass various dimensions of IT service management, including incident management, problem management, change management, service level management, and more. Evaluate the maturity and effectiveness of each process by analyzing data and metrics, conducting interviews, and gathering feedback from stakeholders and end-users. This comprehensive evaluation will help identify bottlenecks, inefficiencies, and areas where automation, standardization, and process improvement can be applied.

Once the assessment is complete, it is essential to prioritize the identified areas for improvement based on their impact and alignment with business goals. This prioritization will guide the implementation of ITIL4 practices in a phased and manageable manner. By focusing on critical areas first, IT professionals can demonstrate value and build momentum for further adoption across the organization.

Implementing ITIL4 in your organization requires a mindset shift from a reactive to a proactive approach. It emphasizes the importance of continual improvement, customer-centricity, and collaboration across departments. Through the adoption of ITIL4's best practices, IT professionals can enhance service quality, reduce downtime, and improve customer satisfaction.

Regular monitoring and measurement of key performance indicators (KPIs) are essential to ensure the effectiveness of ITIL4 implementation. KPIs such as mean time to repair, customer satisfaction scores, and service availability should be continuously tracked and analyzed to measure progress and identify areas that require further attention.

In conclusion, assessing your organization's current IT service management practices is a crucial step toward the successful implementation of ITIL4. By identifying areas for improvement and prioritizing their implementation, IT professionals can enhance service delivery, align IT with business objectives, and drive overall organizational success in today's digital age.

Steps to assessing your organization's current IT Service Management (ITSM) practices

Assessing your organization's current IT service management (ITSM) practices is a crucial step in the ITIL 4 framework. This assessment helps organizations understand their strengths, weaknesses, and areas for improvement in delivering IT services. The assessment process involves evaluating various aspects of ITSM against ITIL 4 guidelines and best practices. Here's a general overview of how organizations can approach the assessment:

1. Understand ITIL 4 Framework:
   - Ensure that key stakeholders are familiar with the ITIL 4 framework and its principles, practices, and concepts. This understanding is fundamental for conducting a meaningful assessment.

2. Define Assessment Scope and Objectives:
   - Clearly define the scope of the assessment, including the services and processes to be evaluated. Identify specific objectives, such as improving service quality, increasing efficiency, or aligning IT services with business goals.

3. Identify Assessment Criteria:
   - Determine the criteria against which ITSM practices will be assessed. This may include adherence to ITIL principles, effectiveness of pro-

cesses, customer satisfaction, and performance metrics.

4. Engage Stakeholders:

- Involve key stakeholders, including IT staff, management, and customers, in the assessment process. Collect feedback and perspectives from different levels of the organization to gain a comprehensive understanding.

5. Assessment Tools and Techniques:

- Use a combination of tools and techniques to gather data and assess ITSM practices. This may involve surveys, interviews, documentation reviews, and performance metrics analysis. Consider using ITIL 4 maturity models for a structured evaluation.

6. Evaluate Processes and Practices:

- Assess key ITSM processes based on ITIL 4 practices, such as incident management, problem management, change management, and others. Evaluate how well these processes are defined, implemented, monitored, and continuously improved.

7. Review Technology and Tools:

- Evaluate the technology and tools used to support ITSM. Ensure that the tools align with ITIL 4 practices and contribute to the efficiency and effectiveness of service delivery.

8. Assess Cultural and Organizational Aspects:

- Consider organizational culture and factors influencing ITSM, such as leadership support, collaboration, and employee engagement. Cultural alignment with ITIL 4 principles is important for successful implementation.

9. Identify Improvement Opportunities:

- Analyze assessment findings to identify areas for improvement. Prioritize these opportunities based on their impact on service delivery and alignment with organizational objectives.

10. Develop Improvement Plans:

- Based on the assessment results, develop actionable improvement plans. Define specific goals, timelines, and responsibilities for implementing changes to enhance ITSM practices.

11. Monitor and Iterate:

- Continuously monitor the impact of improvements and iterate the assessment process. Regularly revisit and adjust ITSM practices to ensure they remain aligned with business goals and ITIL 4 principles.

Assessing your organization's current ITSM practices is an ongoing and iterative process. It provides a foundation for implementing continuous improvement and ensures that IT services remain aligned with the evolving needs of the business and its stakeholders.

Defining your organization's ITIL4 implementation goals and objectives

In today's fast-paced and ever-evolving digital landscape, IT professionals must stay ahead of the curve and adopt best practices that align with industry standards. One such framework that has gained immense popularity is ITIL4, which stands for Information Technology Infrastructure Library. ITIL4 provides a comprehensive set of guidelines and practices to manage IT services effectively and efficiently, ensuring a seamless alignment between IT and business objectives.

Implementing ITIL4 in your organization can bring about a transformative change, improving the overall productivity, customer satisfaction, and cost-effectiveness of your IT operations. However, embarking on this journey requires careful planning and a clear understanding of your organization's goals and objectives. This section will guide you through the process of defining these goals and objectives to ensure a successful ITIL4 implementation.

The first step in defining your organization's ITIL4 implementation goals is to assess your current IT service management practices and identify areas of improvement. This could involve conducting a comprehensive gap analysis, engaging with key stakeholders, and gaining insights into the pain points and challenges faced by your IT team.

Once you have a clear understanding of your organization's current state, you can start setting specific, measurable, achievable, relevant, and time-bound (SMART) goals for your ITIL4 implementation. These goals should be aligned with your organization's overall strategic objectives, as well as the needs and expectations of your customers.

Some common goals of ITIL4 implementation include enhancing service quality, reducing service downtime, improving response times, increasing customer satisfaction, optimizing resource utilization, and ensuring compliance with regulatory requirements.

In addition to setting goals, it is equally important to define specific objectives that will help you achieve these goals. Objectives are the actionable steps or milestones that will guide your ITIL4 implementation journey. They should be concrete, realistic, and measurable so that progress can be tracked and evaluated.

Throughout this section, you will learn about various techniques and frameworks to define your organization's ITIL4 implementation goals and objectives. These include conducting a SWOT analysis, utilizing the balanced scorecard approach, and leveraging the ITIL4 value chain model.

By clearly defining your organization's ITIL4 implementation goals and objectives, you will be able to create a roadmap that aligns IT services with business objectives, enhances customer satisfaction, and drives continuous improvement. This section will equip you with the knowledge and tools necessary to embark on your ITIL4 implementation journey with confidence and success.

Building a strong business case for ITIL4 adoption

In today's rapidly evolving digital landscape, organizations are under constant pressure to deliver high-quality IT services that align with business objectives. To achieve this, many IT professionals are turning to the IT Infrastructure Library (ITIL) framework, specifically ITIL4, as a strategic approach to managing IT services. However, before embarking on the journey to implement ITIL4 in your organization, it is crucial to build a strong business case that demonstrates the value and benefits it can bring.

The first step in building a business case for ITIL4 adoption is to clearly define the pain points and challenges that your organization is currently facing. Whether it is inefficient service delivery, frequent incidents, or lack of visibility into IT processes, you need to articulate these issues in a way that resonates with key stakeholders. By presenting a comprehensive analysis of the current state of IT services, you can highlight the potential risks and costs of not adopting ITIL4.

Next, it is important to outline the specific benefits that ITIL4 can offer. These benefits include improved service quality, enhanced customer satisfaction, reduced costs, increased productivity, and better alignment with business goals. It is essential to link these benefits directly to the pain points identified earlier, demonstrating how ITIL4 can address and overcome them. By quantifying the potential cost savings and ROI, you can create a compelling argument for ITIL4 adoption.

Once the benefits are established, it is crucial to highlight the potential risks and challenges associated with implementing ITIL4. These may include resistance to change, resource constraints, or the need for additional training. By acknowledging these challenges upfront and presenting a mitigation plan, you can instill confidence in stakeholders and show that you have carefully considered the implementation process.

Furthermore, it is essential to emphasize the industry trends and best practices that support the adoption of ITIL4. Discuss how ITIL4 aligns with other frameworks such as Agile, DevOps, and Lean, and how it can enable your organization to stay competitive in the digital era. By providing evidence from industry experts and successful case studies, you can demonstrate that ITIL4 is not just a theoretical framework, but a proven methodology for IT service management.

Lastly, it is vital to present a roadmap for ITIL4 adoption, outlining the key milestones, timelines, and resource requirements. This will help stakeholders visualize the implementation process and understand the steps involved in achieving the desired outcomes.

In conclusion, building a strong business case for ITIL4 adoption requires a thorough analysis of the organization's pain points, clear articulation of benefits, acknowledgment of risks, and a roadmap for implementation. By presenting a compelling case supported by industry trends and best practices, IT professionals can gain the support and buy-in needed to successfully implement ITIL4 in their organizations.

Chapter 3: Preparing for ITIL4 Implementation

Assembling an ITIL4 implementation team

Implementing ITIL4 in your organization requires a well-structured team with diverse skill sets and expertise. In this section, we will discuss the key steps involved in assembling an effective ITIL4 implementation team, ensuring a successful transition to the new framework.

1. Identify the Key Stakeholders: The first step is to identify the key stakeholders who will be affected by the ITIL4 implementation. This includes individuals from IT, business operations, and management who will provide support, guidance, and resources throughout the process.

2. Define Roles and Responsibilities: Once the stakeholders are identified, it is crucial to define clear roles and responsibilities for each team member. This will help avoid confusion and ensure that everyone understands their contribution towards the implementation.

3. Technical Expertise: Your team should consist of individuals with technical expertise in IT service management. These professionals should possess a thorough understanding of ITIL4 practices, processes, and frameworks. They will be responsible for guiding the implementation and providing technical support to other team members.

4. Change Management Specialists: Change management is a critical aspect of any ITIL4 implementation. Including change management specialists in your team will help ensure that the transition is smooth and that employees embrace the changes effectively.

5. Communication and Training Experts: It is essential to have team members who excel in communication and training. They will be responsible for creating awareness about the ITIL4 implementation, conducting training sessions, and addressing any concerns or queries from employees.

6. Project Management Skills: A well-structured ITIL4 implementation requires effective project management skills. Including individuals with experience in project management will ensure that the implementation is properly planned, executed, and monitored.

7. Continuous Improvement Champions: ITIL4 emphasizes the concept of continuous improvement. Having team members with a passion for innovation and improvement will help drive the organization's journey toward excellence.

8. Cross-Functional Collaboration: Finally, ensure that your team consists of individuals from various departments, fostering cross-functional collaboration. This will enable a holistic approach to the implementation process and help align ITIL4 practices with the overall organizational goals.

By assembling an ITIL4 implementation team with the right skill sets and expertise, your organization will be well-equipped to embrace the new framework. Remember, effective teamwork is the key to a successful transition, and this section has provided you with a clear roadmap to build your dream team.

Conducting a gap analysis and identifying areas for improvement

In the fast-paced and ever-evolving world of IT, organizations must continuously strive to improve their processes and services to stay ahead of the competition. Implementing ITIL4, the latest version of the IT Infrastructure Library, is a crucial step towards achieving this goal. This section aims to guide IT professionals on how to conduct a gap analysis and identify areas for improvement when implementing ITIL4 in their organization.

A gap analysis is a systematic approach that helps organizations identify the difference between their current state and the desired future state. By conducting a thorough gap analysis, IT professionals can gain valuable insights into the areas that require improvement to align with ITIL4 best practices.

The first step in conducting a gap analysis is to establish a clear understanding of the organization's current processes and practices. This can be achieved through documentation and interviews with key stakeholders. By mapping out the existing processes, IT professionals can identify gaps and areas that need improvement.

Once the current state has been established, the next step is to define the desired future state based on the ITIL4 framework. This involves studying the ITIL4 documentation and identifying the processes, roles, and functions that need to be implemented or improved upon.

After defining the future state, the actual gap analysis begins. This involves comparing the current state with the desired future state and identifying the gaps. These gaps can be categorized into various areas, such as processes, roles, technology, or resources.

Once the gaps have been identified, IT professionals can prioritize them based on their impact and feasibility. Prioritization helps ensure that the most critical areas are addressed first, maximizing the benefits of the ITIL4 implementation.

Once the gaps have been prioritized, the next step is to develop an action plan to bridge these gaps. This plan should include specific activities, timelines, responsibilities, and resources required for each gap. Regular progress monitoring and reporting should also be established to track the implementation of the action plan.

In conclusion, conducting a gap analysis and identifying areas for improvement is a crucial step in implementing ITIL4 in your organization. By following a systematic approach, IT professionals can gain valuable insights into their current processes and practices and align them with ITIL4 best practices. This will ultimately lead to improved service delivery, increased customer satisfaction, and a competitive edge in the IT industry.

Developing an implementation roadmap and timeline

As IT professionals, the successful implementation of ITIL4 in your organization requires careful planning and a well-defined roadmap. Developing an implementation roadmap and timeline is crucial to ensure a smooth transition and maximize the benefits of ITIL4.

The first step in developing an implementation roadmap is to assess your organization's current IT service management (ITSM) capabilities. This assessment will help you identify the gaps and areas that need improvement. It is essential to conduct a thorough analysis of your organization's processes, tools, and resources to determine the scope and scale of the implementation project.

Once you have a clear understanding of your organization's current state, the next step is to define the desired future state. This involves setting specific objectives and goals that align with your organization's overall business strategy. It is important to involve key stakeholders and decision-makers in this process to ensure their buy-in and support throughout the implementation journey.

With the current and future states defined, you can now start developing the implementation roadmap. The roadmap should outline the necessary steps, activities, and milestones required to achieve the desired future state. It should include a detailed timeline that specifies when each step will be executed, allowing for realistic deadlines and resource allocation.

When developing the roadmap, it is crucial to prioritize the implementation activities based on their impact and dependencies. Some activities may need to be completed before others can start, while others can be conducted simultaneously. By prioritizing and sequencing the activities, you can ensure a logical flow and minimize disruptions to ongoing operations.

It is also important to consider the organizational change management aspect of the implementation. ITIL4 introduces new processes and ways of working, which may require a cultural shift within your organization. Developing a change management plan that includes communication, training, and stakeholder engagement will help ensure a smooth transition and acceptance of the changes.

Throughout the implementation process, it is crucial to regularly review and update the roadmap and timeline as needed. This allows for flexibility and adjustment based on new insights, challenges, and resource availability. Regular communication and collaboration with key stakeholders will help maintain their support and address any concerns or issues that arise.

In conclusion, developing an implementation roadmap and timeline is a critical step in successfully implementing ITIL4 in your organization. It provides a clear path forward and ensures that the implementation activities are well-planned, prioritized, and executed. By involving key stakeholders and considering change management, you can navigate the implementation journey smoothly and maximize the benefits of ITIL4 for your organization.

Step-by-step implementation roadmap template

Implementing ITIL 4 involves a systematic approach to aligning IT service management practices with organizational goals and improving service delivery. Here's a general ITIL 4 implementation roadmap that organizations can follow:

1. Assessment and Readiness:

- Conduct an initial assessment of the current state of IT service management practices.

- Identify key stakeholders and gain their support for the ITIL 4 implementation.

- Assess the organization's readiness for change and identify potential challenges.

2. Education and Training:

- Provide education and training sessions on ITIL 4 principles, practices, and concepts.

- Ensure that relevant staff members are familiar with the ITIL 4 framework.

- Consider certification programs for key personnel to build expertise.

3. Define Scope and Objectives:

- Clearly define the scope of the ITIL 4 implementation.

- Set specific and measurable objectives aligned with business goals.

- Identify key performance indicators (KPIs) to measure success.

4. Establish a Governance Framework:

- Define a governance framework that includes policies, roles, and responsibilities.

- Establish a Change Advisory Board (CAB) and other governance bodies as needed.
- Develop guidelines for decision-making and accountability.

5. Select and Customize ITIL Practices:
- Select ITIL 4 practices that are relevant to the organization's needs.
- Customize selected practices to fit the organization's context and culture.
- Develop documented procedures and workflows for the chosen practices.

6. Implement Service Value System (SVS):
- Introduce the Service Value System (SVS) as the overarching framework.
- Implement the Service Value Chain (SVC) activities: Plan, Improve, Engage, Design & Transition, Obtain/Build, and Deliver & Support.
- Align ITIL 4 practices with the SVS and SVC for seamless integration.

7. Implement Guiding Principles:
- Embed the seven guiding principles of ITIL 4 into decision-making processes.
- Encourage a cultural shift based on the guiding principles.
- Apply the principles consistently across the organization.

8. Develop and Implement a Communication Plan:
- Develop a communication plan to keep stakeholders informed.
- Communicate the benefits of ITIL 4 adoption and how it aligns with organizational objectives.
- Address any concerns or resistance through transparent communication.

9. Pilot Implementation:

- Conduct a pilot implementation of ITIL 4 practices in a controlled environment.
- Gather feedback from users and stakeholders to identify improvements.
- Adjust processes and documentation based on lessons learned.

10. Scale and Rollout:

- Expand the implementation to other areas of the organization.
- Monitor performance metrics and KPIs to assess the impact.
- Continuously optimize and scale the implementation based on feedback and results.

11. Continuous Improvement:

- Establish a culture of continuous improvement.
- Regularly review and assess the effectiveness of ITIL 4 practices.
- Identify opportunities for enhancement and adjust the implementation accordingly.

12. Monitoring and Reporting:

- Implement monitoring and reporting mechanisms to track the success of ITIL 4 adoption.
- Generate regular reports on key performance indicators and achievements.
- Share progress with stakeholders to maintain visibility and support.

13. Audit and Certification:

- Conduct periodic audits to ensure compliance with ITIL 4 practices.
- Consider obtaining ITIL 4 certifications for relevant personnel.
- Use audit results to further refine and improve the implementation.

14. Documentation and Knowledge Management:

- Document ITIL 4 practices, processes, and improvements.
- Implement knowledge management practices to capture and share lessons learned.
- Ensure that documentation is accessible and up-to-date.

15. Sustain and Evolve:

- Sustain the ITIL 4 implementation by embedding practices into daily operations.
- Evolve the implementation based on changing business needs and industry trends.
- Foster a culture of innovation and adaptability.

By following this ITIL 4 implementation roadmap, organizations can systematically integrate ITIL 4 principles and practices, ultimately enhancing the efficiency, effectiveness, and value of their IT service management processes.

Chapter 4: ITIL4 Service Strategy

Understanding the key concepts of service strategy

As IT professionals, it is crucial to stay updated with the latest frameworks and methodologies that can enhance the efficiency and effectiveness of our organizations. One such framework that has gained immense popularity is ITIL4 (Information Technology Infrastructure Library version 4). In this section, we will delve into the key concepts of service strategy, a fundamental aspect of ITIL4, and understand how it can be implemented in your organization.

Service strategy, as the name suggests, is the phase of ITIL4 that focuses on defining and developing a strategic approach to delivering IT services. It helps organizations align their IT services with business objectives, ultimately leading to improved customer satisfaction and organizational success. To implement service strategy effectively, IT professionals need to grasp the key concepts that underpin this phase.

The first key concept is defining value. Service strategy emphasizes the importance of understanding and delivering value to customers. It involves identifying what the customers perceive as valuable and aligning IT services accordingly. By focusing on value, organizations can ensure that their IT services are meeting the needs and expectations of their customers.

Another crucial concept is service assets. Service assets refer to the resources and capabilities that an organization possesses to deliver value to its customers. These assets can include people, processes, technology, and information. Service strategy helps IT professionals identify and leverage these assets to create and deliver IT services that align with customer value.

Service portfolio management is yet another key concept. It involves managing the entire lifecycle of services, from conceptualization to retirement. This concept helps IT professionals make informed decisions regarding which services to invest in, develop, and retire based on their alignment with business objectives and customer value.

Lastly, financial management is a vital aspect of service strategy. IT professionals need to understand the financial implications of their decisions and ensure that resources are allocated effectively. By practicing financial management, organizations can optimize their IT investments and ensure that the allocated budget is utilized most efficiently.

In conclusion, understanding the key concepts of service strategy is essential for IT professionals looking to implement ITIL4 in their organizations. By grasping the concepts of defining value, managing service assets, service portfolio management, and financial management, IT professionals can align their IT services with business objectives and deliver value to their customers. This section provides a comprehensive overview of these concepts and equips IT professionals with the knowledge and insights necessary to successfully implement service strategy in their organizations.

Defining your organization's service strategy

Defining your organization's service strategy is a critical step in implementing ITIL4 within your organization. The service strategy is the foundation for all other aspects of IT service management, and it sets the direction and goals for the organization.

To start, it is essential to understand what service strategy means in the context of ITIL4. Service strategy is about identifying and defining the services that the organization will offer to its customers. It involves understanding the needs and requirements of the customers and aligning the services with the organization's overall business objectives.

One of the key elements of defining service strategy is conducting a thorough analysis of the organization's internal and external environments. This analysis helps identify the organization's strengths, weaknesses, opportunities, and threats. It also helps in understanding the market dynamics and the competition.

Another important aspect of service strategy is defining the value proposition for the customers. This involves understanding what value the services will bring to the customers and how they will differentiate the organization from its competitors. The value proposition should be clear, compelling, and aligned with the organization's overall business strategy.

Defining the service portfolio is another crucial step in service strategy. The service portfolio includes all the services that the organization currently offers, plans to offer in the future, or has retired. It provides a comprehensive view of the services and helps in making informed decisions about service offerings and investments.

Furthermore, service strategy involves defining the financial management processes and mechanisms for managing the costs and investments associated with the services. This includes setting the service pricing strategy, defining the cost models, and establishing the budgeting and accounting practices.

Lastly, service strategy also includes defining the governance and risk management processes. This ensures that the services are delivered in a controlled and compliant manner, and any potential risks are identified and mitigated.

In conclusion, defining your organization's service strategy is a crucial step in implementing ITIL4. It involves understanding the organization's internal and external environments, defining the value proposition, creating a service portfolio, establishing financial management processes, and defining governance and risk management processes. By defining a robust service strategy, IT professionals can align the services with the organization's business objectives and deliver value to the customers.

Step-by-step roadmap for Service Strategy

Developing a Service Strategy is a critical component of the ITIL 4 framework, as it sets the direction for the organization and aligns IT services with business goals. Here's a step-by-step roadmap to guide the implementation of ITIL 4 Service Strategy:

1. Understand Business Objectives:
   - Objective: Gain a deep understanding of the overall business strategy and objectives.
   - Activities:
   - Engage with key stakeholders, including business leaders and executives.
   - Analyze business plans, goals, and priorities.

2. Conduct a Service Provider Analysis:
   - Objective: Assess the organization's capabilities and resources to deliver services.
   - Activities:
   - Evaluate the current state of IT services, technologies, and infrastructure.
   - Assess the organization's strengths, weaknesses, opportunities, and threats (SWOT analysis).

3. Define Market Spaces and Potential Services:
   - Objective: Identify potential areas for service offerings that align with business needs.
   - Activities:
   - Analyze market trends, customer needs, and industry benchmarks.
   - Explore opportunities for innovation and differentiation.

4. Develop Service Offerings and Packages:
- Objective: Define specific services, service packages, and service levels.
- Activities:
- Specify features, benefits, and value propositions for each service.
- Develop pricing models and service level agreements (SLAs).

5. Establish Service Portfolios:
- Objective: Create a comprehensive portfolio of services to be offered.
- Activities:
- Categorize services into service portfolios based on strategic objectives.
- Define criteria for prioritizing and managing services within the portfolios.

6. Define Service Models:
- Objective: Determine how services will be designed, delivered, and supported.
- Activities:
- Choose appropriate service delivery models (e.g., in-house, outsourced, hybrid).
- Define service design principles and standards.

7. Identify Strategic Risks:
- Objective: Assess potential risks that may impact the successful delivery of services.
- Activities:
- Identify and analyze strategic risks associated with service offerings.
- Develop risk mitigation plans and strategies.

8. Define Governance and Compliance:

- Objective: Establish governance structures to ensure alignment with organizational goals and compliance with regulations.
   - Activities:
   - Define roles and responsibilities within the service strategy.
   - Develop policies and procedures for governance and compliance.

9. Develop Measurement Framework:
   - Objective: Define key performance indicators (KPIs) and metrics to measure the success of service offerings.
   - Activities:
   - Identify critical success factors for each service.
   - Establish a framework for ongoing performance measurement.

10. Create a Communication Plan:
   - Objective: Communicate the Service Strategy to stakeholders and ensure understanding.
   - Activities:
   - Develop a communication plan with targeted messages for different audiences.
   - Conduct workshops, training sessions, and presentations to disseminate information.

11. Review and Validate:
   - Objective: Validate the Service Strategy with key stakeholders and make necessary adjustments.
   - Activities:
   - Conduct reviews with business leaders, IT teams, and other relevant stakeholders.
   - Incorporate feedback and make refinements to the Service Strategy.

12. Document the Service Strategy:

- Objective: Document the Service Strategy to serve as a reference for implementation and ongoing management.
- Activities:
- Create comprehensive documentation that outlines each aspect of the Service Strategy.
- Ensure documentation is accessible and regularly updated.

13. Implement and Monitor:

- Objective: Implement the Service Strategy and continuously monitor its effectiveness.
- Activities:
- Execute the plan for introducing new services and updating existing ones.
- Monitor performance against defined KPIs and make adjustments as needed.

14. Continual Improvement:

- Objective: Establish a culture of continual improvement for the Service Strategy.
- Activities:
- Regularly review feedback, performance metrics, and industry trends.
- Identify opportunities for improvement and update the Service Strategy accordingly.

By following this step-by-step roadmap, organizations can systematically develop and implement an ITIL 4 Service Strategy that aligns IT services with business objectives, delivers value, and supports ongoing improvement.

Aligning service strategy with business objectives

Aligning service strategy with business objectives is crucial for organizations looking to implement ITIL4. In today's rapidly evolving digital landscape, IT professionals are constantly challenged to align their service strategies with the overall business objectives of their organizations. This section aims to provide a step-by-step guide for IT professionals to effectively align their service strategies with their organization's business goals.

To begin with, it is important to understand that the service strategy is the foundation of the ITIL4 framework. It helps organizations define the value they want to create and deliver to their customers. By aligning the service strategy with business objectives, IT professionals can ensure that their efforts are contributing to the overall success of the organization.

The first step in aligning service strategy with business objectives is to clearly define and understand the business goals and objectives. This involves working closely with key stakeholders and conducting thorough analysis to identify the organization's strategic priorities. By having a clear understanding of the business objectives, IT professionals can align their service strategies accordingly.

The next step is to assess the organization's current IT capabilities and identify any gaps that need to be addressed. This involves conducting a thorough assessment of the IT infrastructure, processes, and resources. By identifying the gaps, IT professionals can develop strategies to bridge them and ensure that the IT capabilities are aligned with the business objectives.

Once the gaps are identified, the next step is to develop a service strategy that aligns with the business objectives. This involves defining the services that need to be delivered, the value they will provide to the customers, and the resources required to deliver these services. It also involves setting clear goals and objectives for each service and establishing metrics to measure their success.

Finally, IT professionals need to continuously monitor and evaluate the service strategy to ensure that it remains aligned with the business objectives. This involves regularly reviewing the performance metrics, gathering feedback from customers, and making necessary adjustments to the strategy if required.

In conclusion, aligning service strategy with business objectives is essential for IT professionals looking to implement ITIL4 in their organizations. By following the step-by-step guide outlined in this section, IT professionals can ensure that their service strategies are in sync with the overall goals and objectives of the organization. This alignment will not only contribute to the success of the organization but also enhance IT service delivery and customer satisfaction.

Chapter 5: ITIL4 Service Design

Understanding the key concepts of service design

In today's rapidly evolving technology landscape, IT professionals face the challenge of delivering high-quality services that meet the ever-changing needs of their organizations. To stay ahead of the curve, it is crucial to adopt a comprehensive framework that not only addresses the current requirements but also enables future growth. ITIL4, a globally recognized IT service management framework, provides organizations with the necessary tools and guidelines to effectively design and deliver services that align with business objectives.

Service design is a critical component of the ITIL4 framework, focusing on the creation and improvement of services to meet customer needs. This section aims to familiarize IT professionals with the key concepts of service design and provide practical insights on how to implement ITIL4 in their organizations.

One of the fundamental concepts in service design is the Service Value System (SVS). The SVS represents the holistic approach to service management and consists of various components, such as guiding principles, governance, and continual improvement. Understanding the SVS is essential as it provides the foundation for designing and delivering valuable services to customers.

Another key concept is the Service Value Chain (SVC), which outlines the activities required to design, develop, and deliver services. The SVC encompasses six core activities: plan, improve, engage, design and transition, obtain/build, and deliver and support. By understanding each activity and its interdependencies, IT professionals can optimize their service design processes and enhance service delivery efficiency.

Furthermore, this section delves into the concept of service offering and agreement, emphasizing the importance of defining clear service offerings and establishing robust agreements with customers. Effective service offering and agreement processes ensure that customers' needs are met, expectations are managed, and service level agreements (SLAs) are aligned with organizational goals.

Additionally, the section explores the concept of service design packages (SDPs), which document the design specifications for new or changed services. IT professionals will learn how to create comprehensive SDPs that capture all necessary information, including service requirements, resource considerations, and risk assessments. Well-defined SDPs contribute to successful service design and enable efficient service transition and implementation.

In conclusion, understanding the key concepts of service design is essential for IT professionals aiming to implement ITIL4 in their organizations. By embracing the concepts of SVS, SVC, service offering and agreement, and SDPs, IT professionals can enhance their service design capabilities and deliver valuable services that align with business objectives.

Creating and documenting service design packages

In today's fast-paced and ever-changing IT landscape, organizations must have a robust and efficient service design process in place. This section explores the concept of creating and documenting service design packages, providing IT professionals with a step-by-step guide on how to implement ITIL4 in their organization.

A service design package (SDP) is a comprehensive document that outlines the design specifications and requirements for a service or service improvement. It serves as a vital communication tool between the service design team and other stakeholders involved in the service lifecycle. By creating and documenting SDPs, organizations can ensure that all aspects of the service design are clearly defined, understood, and aligned with business objectives.

The first step in creating an SDP is to identify the service requirements and objectives. This involves gathering input from various stakeholders, including business users, customers, and IT staff. By understanding their needs and expectations, IT professionals can design services that meet these requirements and add value to the organization.

Once the service requirements are defined, the next step is to document the service design. This includes capturing the design specifications, service levels, and performance targets. IT professionals must also consider factors such as capacity, availability, and security when designing the service. The documentation should be detailed and comprehensive, providing a clear roadmap for service implementation and management.

In addition to design specifications, the SDP should also include information on service transition and service operation. This ensures that the service design is aligned with the overall service lifecycle and can be effectively implemented and managed. IT professionals should consider factors such as service testing, training, and service desk support when documenting these aspects.

To ensure the effectiveness of the SDP, it is essential to review and validate the design with key stakeholders. This allows for feedback and ensures that the design meets the requirements and expectations of the organization. Regular reviews and updates of the SDP are also necessary to accommodate changes in business needs and technology advancements.

In conclusion, creating and documenting service design packages is a critical step in implementing ITIL4 in your organization. By following a systematic approach and involving key stakeholders, IT professionals can ensure that the service design is aligned with business objectives and meets the needs of the organization. The SDP serves as a valuable tool in communicating the design specifications and requirements, enabling successful service implementation and management.

Managing service design changes and improvements

Managing service design changes and improvements is a crucial aspect of implementing ITIL4 in your organization. In this section, we will explore the best practices and strategies for effectively handling changes and improvements in service design.

Service design changes and improvements are inevitable in any IT organization. As technology evolves and business requirements change, it becomes essential to adapt and enhance service design to meet the evolving needs of the organization and its customers. However, managing these changes and improvements can be a complex task that requires careful planning, coordination, and communication.

One of the key aspects of managing service design changes and improvements is having a robust change management process in place. This process should include clear roles and responsibilities, defined change categories, and a well-defined change request and approval process. By having a structured change management process, you can ensure that all changes are properly assessed, prioritized, and implemented in a controlled and coordinated manner.

Another important aspect is conducting thorough impact assessments before implementing any changes or improvements. This involves analyzing the potential risks, costs, and benefits associated with the proposed changes. By conducting impact assessments, you can identify any potential issues or challenges that may arise and develop appropriate mitigation strategies.

Furthermore, it is crucial to involve key stakeholders and subject matter experts in the change and improvement process. By including their input and expertise, you can ensure that the changes align with the organization's goals and objectives, as well as meet the needs of the customers. Collaboration and communication are key to successful service design changes and improvements.

Additionally, it is essential to monitor and measure the effectiveness of the implemented changes and improvements. This can be done through regular service reviews, customer feedback, and performance metrics. By monitoring the results, you can identify any areas that require further adjustments or improvements.

In conclusion, managing service design changes and improvements is a critical aspect of implementing ITIL4 in your organization. By following best practices and strategies, such as having a robust change management process, conducting impact assessments, involving key stakeholders, and monitoring the results, you can ensure that the changes and improvements are implemented successfully and contribute to the overall success of your IT services.

Step-by-step roadmap to guide the implementation of Service Design

Implementing a Service Design within the ITIL 4 framework involves creating services that meet business needs and align with the overall strategy. Here's a step-by-step roadmap to guide the implementation of ITIL 4 Service Design:

1. Understand Service Requirements:
   - Objective: Gain a clear understanding of business requirements and user needs.
   - Activities:
   - Engage with stakeholders to gather and document service requirements.
   - Analyze business processes and objectives to identify service design

criteria.

2. Define Service Scope and Constraints:
 - Objective: Clearly define the scope of the service and any constraints that may impact its design.
 - Activities:
 - Identify and document the boundaries of the service.
 - Determine any limitations or constraints on service design.

3. Create a Service Design Package (SDP):
 - Objective: Develop a comprehensive documentation package for the service.
 - Activities:
 - Document service requirements, design specifications, and con-straints.
 - Include information on service levels, security, capacity, and continuity.

4. Define Service Level Agreements (SLAs):
 - Objective: Establish clear SLAs that define the expected level of service performance.
 - Activities:
 - Work with stakeholders to define measurable SLAs.
 - Document SLAs in the Service Design Package.

5. Design the Service Architecture:
 - Objective: Create a detailed service architecture that outlines the structure and components of the service.
 - Activities:
 - Define the technical and organizational components of the service.
 - Consider scalability, availability, and performance requirements.

6. Identify and Manage Risks:

- Objective: Identify potential risks to the service and develop strategies for risk management.
- Activities:
- Conduct a risk assessment to identify threats and vulnerabilities.
- Develop risk mitigation plans and incorporate them into the Service Design Package.

7. Define Service Continuity and Availability:

- Objective: Ensure that the service can continue to operate in the event of disruptions.
- Activities:
- Develop a service continuity plan to address potential service interruptions.
- Define availability requirements and strategies.

8. Security and Compliance Considerations:

- Objective: Address security and compliance requirements for the service.
- Activities:
- Identify security measures and controls.
- Ensure that the service design complies with relevant regulations and standards.

9. Consider Supplier and Partner Relationships:

- Objective: Identify and establish relationships with external suppliers and partners.
- Activities:
- Define roles and responsibilities for external parties.
- Establish agreements and contracts as needed.

10. Design the User Experience:
  - Objective: Consider the end-user experience and ensure usability.
  - Activities:
  - Design user interfaces and interactions.
  - Conduct usability testing to validate design decisions.

11. Document Service Design:
  - Objective: Document the entire service design in detail.
  - Activities:
  - Update the Service Design Package with all relevant information.
  - Ensure that documentation is accessible and regularly maintained.

12. Review and Validate:
  - Objective: Validate the service design with key stakeholders and make necessary adjustments.
  - Activities:
  - Conduct reviews with business leaders, IT teams, and other relevant stakeholders.
  - Incorporate feedback and make refinements to the service design.

13. Create Transition Plans:
  - Objective: Develop plans for transitioning the service from design to deployment.
  - Activities:
  - Identify key transition activities and milestones.
  - Develop a rollout plan and communicate it to relevant stakeholders.

14. Implement and Monitor:
  - Objective: Implement the service design and monitor its performance.
  - Activities:

- Execute the rollout plan and deploy the service.
- Monitor performance against SLAs and other key metrics.

15. Continual Improvement:
  - Objective: Establish a culture of continual improvement for the service design.
  - Activities:
  - Regularly review feedback, performance metrics, and user experiences.
  - Identify opportunities for improvement and update the service design accordingly.

By following this step-by-step roadmap, organizations can systematically design and implement ITIL 4 Service Design, ensuring that services are aligned with business requirements, effectively meet user needs, and are positioned for ongoing improvement.

Chapter 6: ITIL4 Service Transition

Understanding the key concepts of service transition

In the world of IT service management, service transition plays a vital role in ensuring the smooth and efficient delivery of services to end-users. It is a critical phase that bridges the gap between service design and service operation. Understanding the key concepts of service transition is essential for IT professionals looking to implement ITIL4 in their organizations.

First and foremost, service transition is all about managing change effectively. It involves transitioning new or changed services into the live environment, while minimizing disruption and maximizing value for both the organization and its customers. To achieve this, several key concepts need to be understood:

1. Change Management: Change is inevitable in any organization, and effective change management is crucial to ensure that changes are planned, evaluated, and implemented in a controlled manner. IT professionals need to understand the importance of assessing the impact and risks associated with changes, as well as establishing change policies and procedures.

2. Service Asset and Configuration Management: This concept focuses on maintaining accurate and up-to-date information about the configuration of IT assets and services. IT professionals should understand the importance of building and maintaining a configuration management system to support service transition activities.

3. Release and Deployment Management: This concept encompasses the planning, scheduling, and controlling of the movement of releases into the live environment. IT professionals need to be aware of the various release and deployment models, as well as the importance of testing, validation, and communication during this process.

4. Knowledge Management: Knowledge is a valuable asset within any organization, and effective knowledge management is essential for successful service transition. IT professionals should understand the importance of capturing, storing, and sharing knowledge to improve decision-making and enhance service delivery.

5. Service Validation and Testing: This concept involves ensuring that services are fit for purpose and meet the specified requirements before they are deployed. IT professionals need to understand the importance of thorough testing and validation to minimize the risk of service disruptions and ensure a seamless transition.

By understanding these key concepts of service transition, IT professionals can effectively implement ITIL4 in their organizations. They will be equipped to manage change, maintain accurate configuration information, plan and control releases, manage knowledge effectively, and validate and test services. Ultimately, this understanding will contribute to the overall success of service delivery and customer satisfaction within the organization.

Planning and managing service transitions

Planning and managing service transitions are essential steps in implementing ITIL4 in any organization. This section will guide IT professionals in understanding the importance of service transitions and provide a step-by-step approach to successfully manage these transitions.

Service transitions refer to the process of moving a service from the development phase to the operational phase. It involves careful planning, coordination, and communication to ensure a seamless transition and minimize disruptions to the business and end-users. By implementing ITIL4, organizations can optimize their service transitions and improve the overall efficiency and effectiveness of their IT services.

The first step in planning service transitions is to identify the scope and objectives of the transition. This involves assessing the current state of the service, understanding the desired end-state, and defining the required resources, timelines, and deliverables. This step lays the foundation for the entire transition process and ensures that all stakeholders have a clear understanding of the goals and expectations.

Next, IT professionals need to develop a detailed transition plan. This plan should include a comprehensive timeline, a breakdown of tasks and responsibilities, and a communication strategy. It is crucial to involve all relevant stakeholders, such as the service owners, development teams, and operational teams, in the planning process. This collaborative approach ensures that everyone is aligned and working towards a common goal.

Once the transition plan is in place, the focus shifts to managing the actual transition. This involves coordinating and executing the planned activities, such as testing, training, and deployment. Effective communication is crucial during this phase to keep all stakeholders informed about the progress and address any issues or concerns that may arise.

Throughout the transition process, IT professionals should also prioritize managing risks and implementing change control mechanisms. This ensures that any potential risks or disruptions are identified and mitigated proactively. Change management processes should be followed to assess the impact of changes, obtain approvals, and schedule them appropriately.

After the transition is complete, it is essential to evaluate and measure the success of the transition. This includes conducting post-implementation reviews and gathering feedback from end-users and stakeholders. These insights can be used to identify areas for improvement and make necessary adjustments to optimize future transitions.

In conclusion, planning and managing service transitions are critical components of implementing ITIL4 in any organization. By following a systematic and collaborative approach, IT professionals can ensure a smooth and successful transition, resulting in improved IT service delivery and customer satisfaction.

Conducting service transition reviews and evaluations

Conducting service transition reviews and evaluations is a crucial aspect of implementing ITIL4 in any organization. It helps IT professionals evaluate and assess the effectiveness and efficiency of service transition processes, ensuring that they align with the organization's objectives and requirements.

Service transition reviews and evaluations serve as a means to identify areas of improvement, address any issues or challenges, and enhance the overall performance of the service transition activities. By conducting regular reviews and evaluations, IT professionals can gain valuable insights into the strengths and weaknesses of the service transition processes, enabling them to make informed decisions for continuous improvement.

When conducting service transition reviews and evaluations, IT professionals should consider several key factors. Firstly, they should establish clear objectives and criteria for evaluation. These objectives should align with the organization's goals and help determine the success of the service transition processes. By defining specific criteria, IT professionals can measure the performance of the processes against predefined benchmarks.

Additionally, it is essential to involve stakeholders from various departments and levels within the organization. This ensures that different perspectives are considered and that the evaluation process remains comprehensive and unbiased. By involving stakeholders, IT professionals can gather valuable feedback and insights that can help identify areas of improvement and address any concerns or issues.

During the evaluation process, IT professionals should collect and analyze relevant data and metrics. This data may include performance indicators, customer feedback, and incident reports. By analyzing this information, IT professionals can gain a comprehensive understanding of the service transition processes' strengths and weaknesses, enabling them to make data-driven decisions for improvement.

Furthermore, it is crucial to document the findings and recommendations from the service transition reviews and evaluations. This documentation serves as a valuable reference for future assessments and allows IT professionals to track progress over time. It also ensures that the organization has a record of the improvements made and the impact they have had on service transition processes.

In conclusion, conducting service transition reviews and evaluations is a vital step in implementing ITIL4 in any organization. By evaluating the effectiveness and efficiency of service transition processes, IT professionals can identify areas of improvement, address challenges, and enhance overall performance. By establishing clear objectives, involving stakeholders, analyzing relevant data, and documenting findings, IT professionals can ensure continuous improvement and alignment with the organization's objectives.

Step-by-step roadmap for implementing Service Transition

The Service Transition stage in ITIL 4 focuses on effectively transition-ing new or changed services into the live environment while managing risks and ensuring minimal disruption. Here's a step-by-step roadmap for implementing ITIL 4 Service Transition:

1. Initiate the Transition Planning and Support:
   - Objective: Establish the groundwork for the transition process.
   - Activities:
   - Define roles and responsibilities for the transition team.
   - Develop a transition plan outlining key activities and timelines.

2. Establish Change Control:
   - Objective: Implement a formalized change control process to manage and authorize changes.
   - Activities:
   - Define change categories and classifications.
   - Establish a Change Advisory Board (CAB) to assess and approve changes.

3. Define Service Asset and Configuration Management:
   - Objective: Establish processes for managing configuration items and assets.
   - Activities:
   - Identify and document configuration items (CIs).
   - Establish a Configuration Management Database (CMDB) and populate it with CI information.

4. Plan and Manage Service Validation and Testing:

- Objective: Ensure that services are thoroughly tested before transition.
- Activities:
- Develop a comprehensive testing strategy.
- Conduct validation and testing activities, including user acceptance testing (UAT).

5. Evaluate and Manage Risks:

- Objective: Identify and manage risks associated with the transition.
- Activities:
- Conduct a risk assessment for the transition.
- Develop risk mitigation plans and strategies.

6. Plan and Coordinate Release and Deployment:

- Objective: Plan the release of services into the live environment.
- Activities:
- Develop a release plan with detailed deployment schedules.
- Coordinate with stakeholders, including users and support teams.

7. Prepare for Knowledge Management:

- Objective: Establish processes for capturing, organizing, and sharing knowledge.
- Activities:
- Create documentation and knowledge articles for the transition.
- Establish a knowledge sharing platform.

8. Update Service Design and Change Management:

- Objective: Ensure that any changes to the service design are documented and communicated.
- Activities:

- Update the Service Design Package and other relevant documentation.
- Communicate changes to stakeholders through appropriate channels.

9. Conduct Training and Awareness:
- Objective: Ensure that relevant personnel are trained and aware of
the upcoming transition.
- Activities:
- Provide training on new or changed services and processes.
- Raise awareness of the transition among users and support teams.

10. Review and Validate Transition Plans:
- Objective: Validate the transition plans with key stakeholders.
- Activities:
- Conduct reviews and walkthroughs of transition plans.
- Incorporate feedback and make necessary adjustments.

11. Implement Changes:
- Objective: Execute the approved changes as per the transition plan.
- Activities:
- Deploy new services or changes to existing services.
- Monitor and manage the transition in accordance with the plan.

12. Verify and Validate Service Changes:
- Objective: Ensure that the implemented changes meet the intended
objectives.
- Activities:
- Conduct post-implementation reviews to verify that services are
operating as expected.
- Validate that users and stakeholders are satisfied with the changes.

13. Update Service Knowledge Management:
- Objective: Document knowledge gained during the transition.
- Activities:
- Update knowledge articles and documentation based on lessons learned.
- Capture information that can be useful for future transitions.

14. Review and Close Change Records:
- Objective: Review and close change records related to the transition.
- Activities:
- Assess the success of changes and document outcomes.
- Close change records and update the CMDB.

15. Evaluate Transition Performance:
- Objective: Evaluate the performance of the transition process.
- Activities:
- Analyze key performance indicators (KPIs) related to the transition.
- Identify areas for improvement and lessons learned.

16. Document and Communicate:
- Objective: Document the entire transition process and communicate outcomes.
- Activities:
- Create a comprehensive transition report.
- Share the report with stakeholders and the organization.

17. Continual Improvement:
- Objective: Establish a culture of continual improvement for the Service Transition stage.
- Activities:
- Regularly review feedback, performance metrics, and user experi-

ences.

- Identify opportunities for improvement and update transition processes accordingly.

By following this step-by-step roadmap, organizations can systematically manage the transition of new or changed services, ensuring a smooth deployment and minimizing disruptions to the live environment.

Chapter 7: ITIL4 Service Operation

Understanding the key concepts of service operation

In today's fast-paced digital world, organizations are heavily reliant on IT services to deliver value to their customers. To ensure smooth and efficient operations, IT professionals must understand the key concepts of service operation. This section aims to provide a comprehensive overview of these concepts, helping IT professionals implement ITIL4 in their organizations.

Service operation is a vital stage in the ITIL service lifecycle. It focuses on the day-to-day activities required to deliver and support IT services effectively. This section explores the key concepts that form the foundation of service operation, enabling IT professionals to optimize service delivery and support processes.

One of the fundamental concepts is the Service Desk, which acts as the single point of contact between the IT organization and its users. IT professionals will learn how to establish an efficient Service Desk, ensuring timely response and resolution of user issues. Additionally, they will understand the importance of Incident Management, which involves restoring normal service operation as quickly as possible when incidents occur.

Change Management is another critical concept covered in this section. IT professionals will gain insights into implementing a structured approach to managing changes in the IT environment, minimizing risks and disruptions. They will also explore the concept of Problem Management, which focuses on identifying and addressing the root causes of recurring incidents, preventing them from reoccurring.

Furthermore, IT professionals will delve into the concept of Event Management, which involves monitoring and managing events in the IT infrastructure to ensure proactive detection and resolution of potential issues. They will also understand the significance of Access Management, which ensures authorized users have the right access to IT services and data, while unauthorized access is prevented.

Lastly, this section introduces the concept of Service Operation Processes, which includes Service Request Management, Technical Management, IT Operations Management, and Application Management. IT professionals will gain a comprehensive understanding of these processes and their role in delivering and supporting IT services effectively.

By grasping the key concepts of service operation, IT professionals can implement ITIL4 principles and practices in their organizations. This section provides a step-by-step guide, equipping them with the knowledge and skills to optimize service delivery, enhance customer satisfaction, and drive organizational success in the digital era.

Managing service requests and incidents

Managing service requests and incidents is a crucial aspect of implementing ITIL4 in any organization. In this section, we will delve into the best practices and strategies for effectively managing these requests and incidents, ensuring smooth operations and optimal customer satisfaction.

Service requests are an integral part of IT service management. They encompass various user inquiries, such as password resets, software installations, and hardware replacements. Efficiently handling these requests is essential to meet customer expectations and maintain a high level of service quality.

To begin, organizations should establish a centralized service desk to streamline the management of service requests. This allows for a single point of contact, ensuring that all requests are logged, categorized, and prioritized appropriately. By adopting a ticketing system, IT professionals can track the progress of each request, ensuring timely resolution and efficient communication with end-users.

Another critical element in managing service requests is the creation of a self-service portal. This portal enables users to submit and track their requests independently, reducing the workload on the service desk and empowering users to take charge of their IT needs. Self-service options can be expanded to include knowledge articles, FAQs, and even automated solutions for common issues. This not only enhances customer satisfaction but also frees up IT professionals to focus on more complex tasks.

Moving on to incident management, it is essential to have a well-defined process in place to handle unexpected disruptions in service. Incidents can range from system outages to software crashes, and the key is to minimize their impact on business operations.

A crucial step is to establish clear incident categorization and prioritization criteria. This ensures that incidents are responded to based on their urgency and impact on business continuity. By categorizing incidents, IT professionals can identify recurring issues and proactively implement preventive measures.

Implementing an incident management system, such as an incident ticketing tool, is vital for efficient incident resolution. This system should facilitate incident logging, tracking, and escalation, enabling IT professionals to collaborate effectively and share information regarding the incident's root cause and resolution.

Furthermore, organizations should consider implementing a problem management process to identify and address underlying causes of incidents. This proactive approach helps prevent future incidents, improving overall service quality.

In conclusion, managing service requests and incidents is essential for IT professionals seeking to implement ITIL4 in their organization. By establishing a centralized service desk, adopting self-service options, and implementing efficient incident management processes, organizations can enhance customer satisfaction, minimize service disruptions, and optimize IT service delivery.

Monitoring and optimizing service performance

Monitoring and optimizing service performance is a crucial aspect of implementing ITIL4 in your organization. In this section, we will explore the various techniques and tools that IT professionals can utilize to ensure that their services are performing at their best.

One of the key principles of ITIL4 is the constant monitoring of service performance. This involves regularly assessing the performance of IT services against defined targets and KPIs (Key Performance Indicators). By monitoring these metrics, IT professionals can identify areas that require improvement and take proactive steps to optimize service performance.

To effectively monitor service performance, IT professionals can leverage various tools and techniques. Performance monitoring tools provide real-time insights into service performance, allowing professionals to identify bottlenecks, performance degradation, or any deviations from defined performance targets. These tools can monitor various aspects of service delivery, such as response times, availability, and throughput, providing a comprehensive view of service performance.

In addition to performance monitoring tools, IT professionals can also utilize techniques like capacity planning and trend analysis. Capacity planning involves forecasting future resource requirements based on historical data, growth projections, and business needs. By accurately estimating resource demands, organizations can ensure that services are adequately provisioned, minimizing the risk of performance issues.

Trend analysis, on the other hand, helps identify patterns and anomalies

72

in service performance over time. By analyzing trends, IT profession-als can uncover recurring issues, seasonal variations, or unexpected performance fluctuations. This information can then be used to opti-mize service performance by implementing targeted improvements or proactively addressing potential issues.

Furthermore, IT professionals should establish a robust incident man-agement process to handle service performance issues effectively. This involves promptly identifying and resolving incidents that impact service performance, minimizing downtime, and ensuring a seamless user experience. Incident management processes should include clear roles and responsibilities, well-defined escalation procedures, and efficient communication channels to enable swift resolution of issues.

By closely monitoring service performance, utilizing appropriate tools and techniques, and implementing effective incident management processes, IT professionals can optimize service delivery and ensure that their organization's IT services meet or exceed performance expectations. This section serves as a practical guide for IT professionals looking to implement ITIL4 principles and best practices to enhance service performance in their organization.

Step-by-step roadmap for implementing Service Operation

Implementing Service Operation in the ITIL 4 framework involves managing the day-to-day operation of services efficiently and effectively. Here's a step-by-step roadmap for implementing ITIL 4 Service Operation:

1. Understand Service Operation Objectives:

- Objective: Gain a clear understanding of the objectives and goals of Service Operation.
- Activities:
- Review the organization's overall business and IT strategy.
- Identify key service operation objectives and performance indicators.

2. Establish Incident Management Process:

- Objective: Set up a structured process to respond to and resolve incidents.
- Activities:
- Define incident categories and priorities.
- Establish procedures for incident detection, recording, and resolution.

3. Implement Problem Management:

- Objective: Identify and address the root causes of recurring incidents.
- Activities:
- Establish a problem management process.
- Conduct root cause analysis and implement corrective actions.

4. Set Up Request Fulfillment:

- Objective: Provide a consistent and efficient process for handling service requests.
- Activities:
- Define service request categories.
- Implement workflows for request fulfillment.

5. Establish Event Management:

- Objective: Proactively monitor and manage events that could impact services.
- Activities:
- Implement event detection and monitoring tools.
- Define thresholds and responses for different types of events.

6. Implement Access Management:

- Objective: Ensure authorized users have appropriate access to services and data.
- Activities:
- Define access policies and permissions.
- Establish procedures for granting and revoking access.

7. Develop Service Desk:

- Objective: Establish a single point of contact for users to report issues and request assistance.
- Activities:
- Set up a service desk with defined roles and responsibilities.
- Implement tools for incident logging and tracking.

8. Implement IT Operations Management:

- Objective: Manage the day-to-day IT infrastructure and operations.
- Activities:

- Define and document routine operational procedures.
- Implement tools for configuration management and monitoring.

9. Define and Measure Service Level Agreements (SLAs):
- Objective: Clearly define SLAs to manage service performance and expectations.
- Activities:
- Establish SLAs for key services.
- Define metrics and key performance indicators (KPIs) for measuring service levels.

10. Establish Operational Monitoring and Reporting:
- Objective: Monitor service performance and generate regular reports for management.
- Activities:
- Implement tools for monitoring service performance.
- Define reporting mechanisms for key stakeholders.

11. Implement Knowledge Management:
- Objective: Capture, store, and share knowledge to enhance service operation.
- Activities:
- Establish a knowledge management process.
- Develop a knowledge base for incidents, problems, and known errors.

12. Implement Continual Improvement:
- Objective: Foster a culture of continuous improvement in service operation.
- Activities:
- Regularly review incidents, problems, and performance metrics.

- Identify opportunities for improvement and implement changes.

13. Document Standard Operating Procedures (SOPs):
- Objective: Document and communicate standardized operating procedures.
- Activities:
- Develop SOPs for routine tasks in service operation.
- Ensure that SOPs are accessible and up-to-date.

14. Conduct Training and Awareness Programs:
- Objective: Ensure that staff members are trained and aware of their roles in service operation.
- Activities:
- Provide training on new tools, processes, and procedures.
- Raise awareness of the importance of service operation.

15. Review and Audit Service Operation Processes:
- Objective: Conduct regular reviews and audits to ensure compliance and effectiveness.
- Activities:
- Conduct internal audits of service operation processes.
- Review performance against SLAs and targets.

16. Communicate with Stakeholders:
- Objective: Communicate service operation performance and improvements to stakeholders.
- Activities:
- Regularly communicate with users, management, and other relevant stakeholders.
- Share performance reports and improvement initiatives.

17. Implement Service Operation Automation:

- Objective: Explore opportunities to automate routine tasks and processes.
- Activities:
- Identify tasks suitable for automation.
- Implement automation tools and scripts.

18. Document and Share Lessons Learned:

- Objective: Capture lessons learned from incidents, problems, and improvements.
- Activities:
- Document and share insights gained from service operation activities.
- Use lessons learned to inform future decisions and improvements.

By following this step-by-step roadmap, organizations can systematically implement ITIL 4 Service Operation, ensuring that day-to-day services are delivered efficiently, incidents are promptly resolved, and the overall operation is aligned with business needs and expectations.

Chapter 8: ITIL4 Continual Service Improvement

Understanding the key concepts of continual service improvement

In the fast-paced world of IT, organizations are constantly seeking ways to enhance their services, improve customer satisfaction, and stay ahead of the competition. The IT Infrastructure Library (ITIL) has long been recognized as a leading framework for managing IT service delivery and support. With the release of ITIL4, IT professionals now have an updated and comprehensive guide that addresses the evolving needs of modern businesses.

One of the core components of ITIL4 is Continual Service Improvement (CSI). This section aims to provide IT professionals with a solid understanding of the key concepts of CSI and how to effectively implement them within their organizations.

CSI is a systematic approach to identifying and implementing improvements in IT services. It is based on the principle that there is always room for improvement, and organizations must continuously strive to enhance their services to meet changing business needs. The key concepts of CSI can be summarized as follows:

1. The Deming Cycle: CSI is built around the Plan-Do-Check-Act (PDCA) cycle, also known as the Deming Cycle. This cycle consists of four stages – plan, do, check, and act – and provides a structured approach to implementing improvements.

2. Measurement and Metrics: CSI emphasizes the importance of measuring and monitoring key performance indicators (KPIs) to assess the effectiveness of IT services. By collecting and analyzing data, organizations can identify areas for improvement and make data-driven decisions.

3. Service Level Management: CSI aligns closely with the Service Level Management (SLM) process. SLM ensures that IT services are delivered as per agreed-upon service levels and seeks to improve service quality over time.

4. Continual Improvement Register: A Continual Improvement Register (CIR) is a central repository that captures all improvement ideas, actions, and their status. It serves as a valuable resource for tracking progress and ensuring that improvements are implemented effectively.

Implementing CSI within your organization requires a structured and systematic approach. This section will provide step-by-step guidance on how to establish a CSI program, including defining improvement objectives, identifying improvement opportunities, implementing improvements, and measuring their impact.

By embracing the key concepts of CSI, IT professionals can drive positive change within their organizations. Continual service improvement not only enhances the quality of IT services but also contributes to overall business success. With ITIL4 as your guide, you will be well-equipped to implement CSI and stay ahead in today's dynamic IT landscape.

Establishing a culture of continual service improvement

In today's fast-paced digital world, organizations are constantly striving to enhance their IT service management practices. One of the most effective ways to achieve this is by establishing a culture of continual service improvement (CSI). This section explores the importance of CSI and provides a step-by-step guide for IT professionals looking to implement ITIL4 in their organizations.

CSI is a fundamental aspect of ITIL4, as it focuses on identifying areas for improvement and making incremental changes to enhance the quality of IT services. By fostering a culture of CSI, organizations can ensure that they are continuously adapting to meet the evolving needs of their customers.

The first step in establishing a culture of CSI is to create awareness and understanding among the IT professionals within the organization. This can be achieved through training sessions and workshops that highlight the benefits of CSI and provide practical examples of its implementation. By involving IT professionals from various departments, a holistic approach to service improvement can be achieved.

Next, it is crucial to establish a framework for CSI that aligns with the organization's overall objectives. This framework should include clear goals and objectives, as well as defined roles and responsibilities for all stakeholders involved in the improvement process. By setting measurable targets and assigning accountability, organizations can ensure that the CSI initiatives are taken seriously and given the necessary resources.

Regular monitoring and measurement of key performance indicators (KPIs) is another essential aspect of CSI. By tracking metrics such as customer satisfaction, service availability, and incident response time, IT professionals can identify areas that require improvement and prioritize their efforts accordingly. This data-driven approach enables organizations to make informed decisions and allocate resources effectively.

To foster a culture of CSI, it is essential to encourage collaboration and innovation within the organization. This can be achieved through regular brainstorming sessions, knowledge sharing platforms, and reward programs that recognize and incentivize employees' contributions to service improvement. By creating a supportive and inclusive environment, organizations can tap into the collective knowledge and expertise of their IT professionals.

In conclusion, establishing a culture of continual service improvement is a crucial step towards enhancing IT service management practices. By creating awareness, setting clear goals, monitoring KPIs, and fostering collaboration, organizations can ensure that they are continuously evolving to meet the ever-changing demands of the digital landscape. By implementing ITIL4 and embracing CSI, IT professionals can drive innovation, improve customer satisfaction, and ultimately contribute to the success of their organization.

Using metrics and measurements to drive improvement

As an IT professional, one of your primary goals is to continuously improve the services and processes within your organization. To achieve this, it is crucial to have a clear understanding of how well your IT operations are performing and identify areas that require attention. This is where metrics and measurements play a vital role in driving improvement.

Metrics and measurements provide valuable insights into the performance and effectiveness of your IT services, processes, and activities. They enable you to track and monitor key performance indicators (KPIs), identify trends, and make data-driven decisions to optimize your ITIL4 implementation. By harnessing the power of metrics, you can drive significant improvements within your organization.

When implementing ITIL4 in your organization, it is essential to establish a set of metrics that align with your goals and objectives. These metrics should be specific, measurable, achievable, relevant, and time-bound (SMART). By defining SMART metrics, you can easily track progress and measure the success of your ITIL4 implementation.

One of the key benefits of using metrics and measurements is the ability to identify areas for improvement. By regularly analyzing the data collected through metrics, you can identify bottlenecks, inefficiencies, and areas that require attention. This enables you to take proactive measures to address these issues and enhance the overall performance of your IT services.

Metrics also play a crucial role in establishing a culture of continuous improvement within your organization. By regularly reviewing and sharing metrics with your team, you create transparency and accountability. This encourages your team members to take ownership of their work and strive for better results. Additionally, metrics can serve as a motivation tool, as they provide a tangible way to track progress and celebrate achievements.

To effectively use metrics and measurements, it is crucial to have the right tools and processes in place. Implementing a robust IT service management (ITSM) tool can help automate the collection and analysis of metrics, saving time and effort. Additionally, establishing a regular reporting cadence and using visualizations can help communicate the metrics effectively to stakeholders and facilitate data-driven decision-making.

In conclusion, using metrics and measurements is essential for driving improvement in your ITIL4 implementation. By establishing SMART metrics, regularly analyzing data, and fostering a culture of continuous improvement, you can optimize your IT services and processes. Embrace the power of metrics and take your ITIL4 implementation to new heights.

Chapter 9: ITIL4 and IT Governance

Aligning ITIL4 with IT governance frameworks

In today's rapidly evolving digital landscape, aligning IT service management with IT governance frameworks has become a critical factor for organizations striving to achieve operational excellence and deliver value to their customers. ITIL4, the latest iteration of the IT Infrastructure Library, provides a comprehensive framework for organizations to effectively manage their IT services while ensuring alignment with broader IT governance strategies.

ITIL4 in Action: A Step-by-Step Guide for IT Professionals explores the practical implementation of ITIL4 and its alignment with various IT governance frameworks. This section aims to provide IT professionals with insights and strategies to seamlessly integrate ITIL4 practices within their organization's existing IT governance framework.

One of the key challenges faced by IT professionals is the integration of ITIL4 with other governance frameworks such as COBIT (Control Objectives for Information and Related Technologies) or ISO/IEC 38500. While these frameworks focus on different aspects of IT governance, they are not mutually exclusive. By aligning ITIL4 with these frame-works, organizations can benefit from a holistic approach to IT gover-nance.

The chapter begins by introducing the concept of IT governance and its significance in today's technology-driven business environment. It then explores the core principles and practices of ITIL4, highlighting how they can be integrated with existing governance frameworks to create synergies and maximize value.

The chapter also delves into the practical steps involved in aligning ITIL4 with IT governance frameworks. It provides a step-by-step guide, starting from assessing the organization's current IT governance practices to identifying areas of alignment and designing a roadmap for implementation. It emphasizes the importance of collaboration between IT and business stakeholders to ensure that ITIL4 practices are effectively integrated into the organization's overall governance strategy.

Additionally, the section discusses the benefits of aligning ITIL4 with IT governance frameworks. These include improved decision-making, enhanced risk management, increased operational efficiency, and better alignment of IT services with business objectives. It also highlights the potential challenges and pitfalls that organizations may encounter during the implementation process and provides guidance on how to overcome them.

By aligning ITIL4 with IT governance frameworks, IT professionals can leverage the best practices of both approaches to create a robust and effective IT governance strategy. This section equips IT professionals with the knowledge and tools they need to successfully implement

ITIL4 within their organization, enabling them to drive business value, enhance customer satisfaction, and achieve operational excellence in the digital age.

Integrating ITIL4 practices into your organization's IT governance structure

As an IT professional, you understand the importance of effective IT governance in ensuring that technology aligns with business objectives and delivers value to the organization. ITIL4, the latest version of the IT Infrastructure Library, provides a comprehensive framework for managing IT services and processes. In this section, we will explore how you can integrate ITIL4 practices into your organization's IT governance structure to improve efficiency, enhance service delivery, and optimize resource allocation.

To implement ITIL4 in your organization, you need to first understand the key components of IT governance. This includes defining roles and responsibilities, establishing accountability, setting performance metrics, and aligning IT with business strategies. ITIL4 can help you achieve these objectives by providing a set of best practices and guidelines.

One of the core principles of ITIL4 is the service value system (SVS). The SVS represents the overall governance framework within which all ITIL4 practices operate. By adopting the SVS, you can ensure that IT services are designed, delivered, and improved in a holistic manner, with clear alignment to business goals. This integration of ITIL4 practices into your IT governance structure will enable better decision-making, risk management, and resource allocation.

Furthermore, ITIL4 introduces the concept of the four dimensions of service management: organizations and people, information and technology, partners and suppliers, and value streams and processes. By considering these dimensions, you can gain a comprehensive understanding of the various aspects that influence your organization's IT services. This knowledge will help you identify areas for improvement, optimize processes, and enhance service delivery.

Additionally, ITIL4 emphasizes the importance of continual improvement. By implementing ITIL4 practices into your IT governance structure, you can establish a culture of continuous learning and improvement within your organization. Regular assessments, reviews, and feedback loops will enable you to identify opportunities for enhancement and drive innovation.

In conclusion, integrating ITIL4 practices into your organization's IT governance structure is crucial for IT professionals looking to implement ITIL4 in their organizations. By adopting the service value system, considering the four dimensions of service management, and fostering a culture of continual improvement, you can enhance service delivery, optimize resource allocation, and ensure that IT aligns with business objectives. By following the step-by-step guide provided in this book, you will be well-equipped to successfully integrate ITIL4 into your organization's IT governance structure and drive positive change within your IT department.

Step-by-step roadmap to guide the integration process into an organization's IT governance structure

Integrating ITIL 4 practices into an organization's IT governance structure requires careful planning, collaboration, and communication. Here's a step-by-step roadmap to guide the integration process:

1. Assessment and Alignment:
   - Objective: Understand the current state of IT governance and align it with ITIL 4 practices.
   - Activities:
   - Assess existing governance frameworks, policies, and procedures.
   - Identify areas where ITIL 4 practices can complement or enhance current governance practices.

2. Executive Buy-In and Support:
   - Objective: Gain support from executive leadership for the integration of ITIL 4 practices.
   - Activities:
   - Present the benefits of aligning ITIL 4 with IT governance to executives.
   - Obtain endorsement and commitment to the integration process.

3. Create a Cross-Functional Team:
   - Objective: Form a team with representation from IT, governance, and other relevant departments.
   - Activities:
   - Identify key stakeholders and assemble a cross-functional integration team.

- Ensure diverse perspectives and expertise within the team.

4. Define Governance Objectives and Key Performance Indicators (KPIs):
- Objective: Clearly define governance objectives that align with ITIL 4 practices.
- Activities:
- Collaborate with the integration team to establish specific governance objectives.
- Define KPIs to measure the success of the integration.

5. Map ITIL 4 Practices to Governance Framework:
- Objective: Identify how ITIL 4 practices align with existing governance frameworks.
- Activities:
- Map ITIL 4 practices to relevant governance domains and processes.
- Identify areas of synergy and potential gaps.

6. Customize ITIL 4 Practices:
- Objective: Tailor ITIL 4 practices to fit the organization's specific governance requirements.
- Activities:
- Customize ITIL 4 practices to align with organizational processes and culture.
- Develop guidelines for the adoption of ITIL 4 practices within the governance context.

7. Develop Governance Policies and Procedures:
- Objective: Integrate ITIL 4 practices into governance policies and procedural documentation.
- Activities:

- Update governance policies to incorporate ITIL 4 principles and practices.

- Develop detailed procedures for implementing ITIL 4-aligned governance.

8. Training and Awareness Programs:

- Objective: Ensure that governance stakeholders are trained on ITIL 4 practices.
- Activities:
- Develop training programs to educate governance teams on ITIL 4.
- Raise awareness about the benefits and expected outcomes of the integration.

9. Pilot Integration:

- Objective: Test the integration in a controlled environment before full-scale implementation.
- Activities:
- Select a specific governance area for the pilot integration.
- Monitor and evaluate the effectiveness of the integrated practices.

10. Iterative Implementation:

- Objective: Implement ITIL 4 practices incrementally across the governance structure.
- Activities:
- Roll out ITIL 4 practices to additional governance domains.
- Collect feedback and make iterative improvements.

11. Communication Plan:

- Objective: Communicate the integration progress to stakeholders and the wider organization.
- Activities:

- Develop a communication plan outlining key milestones and updates.

- Share success stories and benefits achieved through the integration.

12. Governance Audits and Assessments:

- Objective: Regularly assess and audit the effectiveness of the
integrated practices.

- Activities:

- Conduct periodic audits to ensure compliance with integrated
practices.

- Assess the impact of ITIL 4 integration on governance outcomes.

13. Feedback Mechanisms:

- Objective: Establish mechanisms for continuous feedback and
improvement.

- Activities:

- Solicit feedback from governance teams and stakeholders.

- Use feedback to refine and enhance the integrated practices.

14. Documentation and Knowledge Management:

- Objective: Document integrated practices and capture lessons
learned.

- Activities:

- Maintain comprehensive documentation of the integrated practices.

- Create a knowledge base for sharing insights and best practices.

15. Evaluate and Optimize:

- Objective: Continuously evaluate the effectiveness of the integrated
practices and optimize as needed.

- Activities:

- Analyze performance metrics and KPIs.

- Identify opportunities for optimization and improvement.

16. Cultural Integration:
- Objective: Foster a culture that embraces ITIL 4 practices within the governance structure.
- Activities:
- Encourage collaboration and knowledge sharing.
- Recognize and celebrate successes related to ITIL 4 integration.

17. Scale and Institutionalize:
- Objective: Scale the integration across the entire organization and institutionalize ITIL 4 practices within the governance framework.
- Activities:
- Expand the integration to cover all governance areas.
- Embed ITIL 4 practices as part of the organization's standard operating procedures.

By following this step-by-step roadmap, organizations can systematically integrate ITIL 4 practices into their IT governance structure, fostering a more aligned and effective approach to managing IT services and delivering value to the business.

Ensuring compliance and accountability with ITIL4

In today's rapidly evolving technology landscape, organizations face numerous challenges when it comes to managing their IT services effectively. With the introduction of ITIL4, IT professionals now have a comprehensive framework that enables them to implement best practices and enhance service delivery across the organization. This section aims to provide a step-by-step guide for IT professionals on ensuring compliance and accountability with ITIL4.

Compliance is a critical aspect of any IT service management framework, and ITIL4 places great emphasis on aligning an organization's practices with its objectives and regulations. By adhering to the guidelines set forth in ITIL4, IT professionals can ensure that their organization's IT services are compliant with industry standards, legal requirements, and internal policies. This not only helps mitigate risks but also builds trust and credibility with stakeholders.

The first step towards ensuring compliance with ITIL4 is to conduct a thorough assessment of the organization's current practices. This involves evaluating existing processes, identifying gaps, and determining areas that require improvement. By doing so, IT professionals can gain a clear understanding of the organization's IT service management maturity level and create a roadmap for implementation.

Once the assessment is complete, IT professionals can begin implementing ITIL4 practices that are relevant to their organization's needs. This may involve defining service management policies, establishing governance structures, and developing robust processes that align with ITIL4 principles. It is crucial to involve key stakeholders throughout this process to ensure buy-in and collaboration.

Accountability is another essential aspect of ITIL4 implementation. IT professionals must establish clear roles and responsibilities within the organization to ensure that everyone understands their obligations and contributes to the success of IT service management. This includes defining roles such as service owners, process owners, and service level managers, and establishing mechanisms to measure and report on performance.

To enhance compliance and accountability, IT professionals should also consider implementing tools and technologies that support ITIL4 practices. This may include IT service management software, automation tools, and reporting systems that provide real-time visibility into service performance and compliance metrics.

Overall, ensuring compliance and accountability with ITIL4 requires a systematic and collaborative approach. By conducting a thorough assessment, implementing relevant practices, establishing clear roles and responsibilities, and leveraging appropriate tools, IT professionals can successfully implement ITIL4 in their organization. This not only improves service delivery but also drives continuous improvement and helps organizations stay ahead in today's competitive business environment.

Chapter 10: ITIL4 and IT Service Management Tools

Evaluating and selecting IT service management tools

As an IT professional looking to implement ITIL4 in your organization, one of the crucial steps is to evaluate and select the right IT service management tools. These tools play a vital role in supporting and enhancing the ITIL4 framework, enabling you to streamline and improve your IT service delivery.

When it comes to evaluating and selecting IT service management tools, there are several factors that you need to consider. Firstly, you need to assess your organization's specific requirements and goals. This includes identifying the key functionalities and features that are essential for your IT service management processes. For example, you might require incident management, change management, or asset management capabilities.

Another important consideration is the scalability and flexibility of the tool. It should be able to accommodate your organization's growth and adapt to changing needs. Look for a tool that can integrate with your existing IT infrastructure and other software applications seamlessly.

Usability is another critical factor. The tool should be intuitive and user-friendly, ensuring that your IT staff can quickly learn and adopt it. A tool with a well-designed user interface and clear navigation will promote efficient and effective use.

Integration capabilities are also essential. Ensure that the tool can integrate with other IT systems and tools that your organization uses. This will enable you to leverage existing investments and avoid unnecessary duplication of efforts.

Furthermore, consider the vendor's reputation and support services. Look for a vendor with a proven track record in providing reliable and responsive support. Check customer reviews and testimonials to get an idea of their customer satisfaction levels.

Cost is another important aspect to evaluate. Determine the total cost of ownership, including the initial purchase cost, licensing fees, and ongoing maintenance and support expenses. Consider both short-term and long-term costs to make an informed decision.

Finally, it is advisable to conduct a proof-of-concept or trial period before making a final selection. This will allow you to test the tool's functionality, performance, and suitability for your organization's specific needs.

Choosing the right IT service management tool is crucial for successful implementation of ITIL4 in your organization. By carefully evaluating and selecting the most suitable tool, you can ensure improved efficiency, better service delivery, and enhanced customer satisfaction.

Implementing ITIL4 practices within your chosen toolset

In today's rapidly evolving digital landscape, IT professionals are constantly seeking ways to improve their organization's IT service management practices. One powerful framework that has gained significant traction is ITIL4 (IT Infrastructure Library version 4). ITIL4 provides a comprehensive set of best practices for managing IT services and aligning them with the needs of the business.

To effectively implement ITIL4 in your organization, it is crucial to leverage the right toolset. The chosen toolset should support and enhance the ITIL4 practices, enabling seamless integration and efficient management of IT services. This section explores the key considerations and steps involved in implementing ITIL4 practices within your chosen toolset.

Firstly, it is important to select a toolset that aligns with the ITIL4 framework. Look for tools that offer comprehensive features and functionalities to support incident management, change management, problem management, service catalog management, and other ITIL4 processes. The toolset should also provide robust reporting and analytics capabilities to monitor and measure the performance of IT services.

Once the toolset is selected, the next step is to customize and configure it to align with your organization's specific ITIL4 requirements. This involves mapping the ITIL4 processes to the toolset's functionalities and defining workflows, roles, and responsibilities accordingly. It is essential to involve key stakeholders and subject matter experts during this process to ensure that the toolset implementation meets the organization's unique needs.

Training and knowledge transfer play a vital role in successfully implementing ITIL4 practices within your chosen toolset. IT professionals should receive comprehensive training on the toolset's functionalities and how it supports the various ITIL4 processes. This will empower them to effectively utilize the toolset and maximize its benefits.

Once the toolset is implemented and the IT professionals are trained, ongoing monitoring and continuous improvement are essential. Regularly evaluate the toolset's performance and gather feedback from users to identify areas for improvement. Continuously update and refine the toolset to ensure it remains aligned with the evolving ITIL4 best practices and the organization's changing needs.

Implementing ITIL4 practices within your chosen toolset is a journey that requires careful planning, collaboration, and ongoing commitment. By leveraging a toolset that aligns with the ITIL4 framework, customizing it to your organization's specific needs, providing comprehensive training, and continuously monitoring and improving, IT professionals can successfully implement ITIL4 in their organization and drive tangible business outcomes.

Maximizing the value of IT service management tools in the ITIL4 context

In today's digital landscape, IT professionals face numerous challenges in managing complex IT service environments. To address these challenges effectively, organizations are increasingly turning to ITIL4, the latest iteration of the IT Infrastructure Library (ITIL) framework. ITIL4 provides a comprehensive set of best practices for IT service management (ITSM), enabling organizations to align their IT services with business objectives and deliver value to customers.

One crucial aspect of implementing ITIL4 successfully is utilizing IT service management tools that support and enhance the framework's practices. These tools play a significant role in streamlining IT service delivery, improving service quality, and enhancing overall organizational efficiency. This section aims to guide IT professionals in maximizing the value of IT service management tools within the ITIL4 context.

Firstly, IT professionals need to understand the key features and capabilities of IT service management tools available in the market. These tools should align with ITIL4 principles and support its key practices, such as incident management, change management, and service level management. By selecting the right toolset, IT professionals can significantly enhance their ability to implement ITIL4 effectively.

Next, IT professionals should consider integrating IT service management tools with other ITIL4 practices and processes. These integrations enable seamless data exchange and process automation, reducing manual effort and minimizing the risk of errors. For example, integrating the incident management module of the IT service management tool with the problem management process can help identify recurring issues and proactively address them.

Furthermore, IT professionals should leverage the reporting and analytics capabilities of IT service management tools to gain insights into the performance of IT services and identify areas for improvement. These tools can generate real-time reports, dashboards, and visualizations, enabling IT professionals to make data-driven decisions and demonstrate the value of IT services to stakeholders.

Lastly, ongoing monitoring and evaluation of IT service management tools' effectiveness are crucial for continuous improvement. IT professionals should regularly assess the tool's usage, user satisfaction, and overall impact on ITIL4 implementation. This evaluation will help identify any gaps or areas for improvement, ensuring the maximum value is derived from the toolset.

In conclusion, maximizing the value of IT service management tools within the ITIL4 context is essential for IT professionals aiming to implement ITIL4 successfully in their organizations. By selecting the right tools, integrating them with other ITIL4 practices, utilizing reporting and analytics capabilities, and continuously evaluating their effectiveness, IT professionals can unlock the full potential of ITIL4 and deliver enhanced IT services that align with business objectives.

Step-by-step guide to evaluating and selecting IT Service Management (ITSM) tools

Evaluating and selecting ITIL 4 IT Service Management (ITSM) tools is a crucial process that involves careful consideration of various factors to ensure that the chosen tools align with organizational needs and goals. Here's a step-by-step guide to help in this process:

1. Define Requirements and Objectives:
- Objective: Clearly define the requirements and objectives for the ITSM tools.
- Activities:
- Engage with key stakeholders to understand their needs.
- Identify specific ITIL 4 practices and processes the tools need to support.
- Define the key objectives such as improving incident management, service request fulfillment, or change management.

2. Create a Cross-Functional Evaluation Team:
- Objective: Assemble a team with representatives from IT, service management, and other relevant departments.
- Activities:
- Ensure diversity in the team, including end-users, administrators, and decision-makers.
- Define roles and responsibilities within the evaluation team.

3. Establish Evaluation Criteria:
- Objective: Define criteria for evaluating ITSM tools.
- Activities:
- Develop a list of features and functionalities required.

- Consider factors such as scalability, ease of use, integration capabilities, reporting, and compliance.

4. Research and Shortlist Vendors:

- Objective: Research and create a shortlist of potential ITSM tool vendors.
- Activities:
- Leverage online reviews, industry reports, and recommendations.
- Consider vendors with a proven track record, positive customer feedback, and a good reputation in the industry.

5. Request for Information (RFI):

- Objective: Gather detailed information from potential vendors.
- Activities:
- Develop an RFI document outlining your organization's requirements.
- Request vendors to provide information about their products, capabilities, and pricing.

6. Vendor Demonstrations:

- Objective: Evaluate vendor capabilities through live demonstrations.
- Activities:
- Schedule demonstrations with shortlisted vendors.
- Focus on how well the tools address specific ITIL 4 practices and meet your defined requirements.

7. Request for Proposal (RFP):

- Objective: Invite detailed proposals from selected vendors.
- Activities:
- Issue an RFP to vendors, including specific details about your organization, requirements, and evaluation criteria.

- Evaluate vendor responses based on completeness, clarity, and alignment with your needs.

8. Evaluate Total Cost of Ownership (TCO):

- Objective: Assess the total cost of implementing and maintaining the ITSM tools.
- Activities:
- Consider not only the initial licensing costs but also implementation, training, support, and ongoing maintenance expenses.
- Evaluate the long-term cost implications of each vendor.

9. Vendor References:

- Objective: Obtain references from other organizations using the ITSM tools.
- Activities:
- Request references from vendors and contact their existing customers.
- Ask about their experiences, challenges faced, and overall satisfaction with the tools.

10. Consider Integration Capabilities:

- Objective: Evaluate the ability of the ITSM tools to integrate with existing and future IT systems.
- Activities:
- Assess integration options with other IT tools, such as monitoring systems, collaboration platforms, and configuration management databases (CMDBs).

11. Scalability and Flexibility:

- Objective: Assess whether the ITSM tools can scale to meet future needs and adapt to changing business requirements.

- Activities:
- Consider the tools' scalability and flexibility in handling growing data, users, and processes.
- Evaluate their ability to accommodate changes in organizational structure and IT practices.

12. Security and Compliance:
- Objective: Ensure that the ITSM tools meet security and compliance requirements.
- Activities:
- Evaluate the tools' security features, data protection mechanisms, and compliance with industry standards.
- Confirm that the vendors follow best practices for security and compliance.

13. Select and Negotiate:
- Objective: Make an informed decision and negotiate the terms with the chosen vendor.
- Activities:
- Select the vendor that best meets your criteria.
- Engage in negotiations regarding pricing, licensing, and contractual terms.

14. Implementation Planning:
- Objective: Develop a detailed plan for the implementation of the selected ITSM tools.
- Activities:
- Collaborate with the vendor to create an implementation roadmap.
- Define roles and responsibilities for both the organization and the vendor.

15. User Training and Adoption:

- Objective: Plan for user training and ensure successful adoption.
- Activities:
- Develop a training program for end-users, administrators, and support staff.
- Promote awareness and facilitate a smooth transition to the new ITSM tools.

16. Monitor and Optimize:

- Objective: Continuously monitor the performance and optimize the use of the ITSM tools.
- Activities:
- Establish key performance indicators (KPIs) for tool usage.
- Regularly review and optimize processes to maximize the benefits of the ITSM tools.

17. Continuous Improvement:

- Objective: Foster a culture of continuous improvement in ITSM processes.
- Activities:
- Encourage feedback from users and administrators.
- Periodically revisit the ITSM tool landscape to identify opportunities for enhancement.

By following this step-by-step guide, organizations can systematically evaluate, select, and implement ITSM tools that align with their needs, ultimately improving service delivery, efficiency, and the overall IT landscape.

Chapter 11: ITIL4 in Action: Case Studies

Case study 1: Successful ITIL4 implementation in a large enterprise

Introduction:

In today's rapidly evolving business landscape, IT professionals face the challenge of aligning IT services with the ever-changing needs of their organizations. To address this, the Information Technology Infrastructure Library (ITIL) has emerged as a globally recognized framework for managing IT service delivery and support. This case study explores the successful implementation of ITIL4 in a large enterprise, providing valuable insights and practical advice for IT professionals looking to implement ITIL4 in their organizations.

Background:

The organization in focus is a multinational corporation operating in multiple industries, with an extensive IT infrastructure supporting its global operations. Prior to the adoption of ITIL4, the IT department faced numerous challenges, including service disruptions, a lack of standardized processes, and inefficient incident management. Recognizing the need for a structured approach to IT service management, the organization embarked on an ITIL4 implementation journey.

Implementation Process:

The implementation process was divided into several key phases. The first step involved conducting a comprehensive assessment of the existing IT service management practices and identifying areas for improvement. This assessment served as a foundation for developing a tailored implementation plan, aligned with the organization's goals and objectives.

Next, the organization formed a dedicated ITIL4 implementation team comprising IT professionals with diverse expertise. This team underwent extensive training and certification in ITIL4, equipping them with the necessary knowledge and skills to drive the implementation process forward.

The implementation team focused on three main areas: service strategy, service design, and service transition. They worked collaboratively with stakeholders across the organization to define service portfolios, establish service level agreements, and streamline change management processes. Additionally, the team introduced a centralized incident management system, enhancing the organization's ability to identify, prioritize, and resolve IT incidents quickly and effectively.

Results and Benefits:

The successful implementation of ITIL4 yielded significant improvements for the organization. Service disruptions were reduced by

40%, resulting in enhanced productivity and customer satisfaction. Standardized processes and procedures led to better resource allocation and improved resource utilization. The incident management system enabled faster response times, reducing downtime and minimizing the impact on business operations.

Conclusion:

This case study exemplifies how a large enterprise successfully implemented ITIL4, resulting in improved IT service management practices and tangible business benefits. For IT professionals looking to implement ITIL4 in their organizations, this case study provides valuable insights and practical guidance. By following a structured implementation process, leveraging a dedicated implementation team, and aligning ITIL4 practices with organizational objectives, IT professionals can drive positive change and unlock the full potential of IT service management in their organizations.

Case study 2: Overcoming challenges during ITIL4 adoption in a small organization

Introduction:

In this section, we will delve into a real-life case study that highlights the challenges faced during the adoption of ITIL4 in a small organization. By examining this case study, IT professionals looking to implement ITIL4 in their organizations will gain valuable insights into the hurdles they may encounter and effective strategies to overcome them.

Background:

The organization in question, a small software development company, recognized the need to adopt ITIL4 principles to enhance service management practices. However, they faced several challenges due to their limited resources, lack of dedicated IT staff, and resistance to change from employees.

Challenge 1: Limited Resources:

The first challenge stemmed from the organization's limited resources. With a small budget, they struggled to allocate funds for training, tools, and infrastructure required for ITIL4 implementation. Additionally, the lack of dedicated IT staff to drive the initiative further complicated matters.

Solution:

To overcome these obstacles, the organization formed a cross-functional team comprising employees from different departments. This team was responsible for researching cost-effective training options, leveraging open-source ITSM tools, and collaborating with external consultants for guidance. By pooling their resources and leveraging their collective expertise, the organization successfully addressed the resource constraints.

Challenge 2: Resistance to Change:

Another significant challenge encountered during ITIL4 adoption was resistance to change from the employees. Many were accustomed to traditional service management practices and were skeptical about the benefits of ITIL4.

Solution:

To address this challenge, the organization implemented a comprehensive change management plan. They conducted awareness sessions, highlighting the advantages of ITIL4 for both individual employees and the organization as a whole. They also provided training and mentoring to help employees understand and embrace the new processes. Regular communication and feedback channels were established to ensure employees felt heard and their concerns were addressed.

Conclusion:

By leveraging a cross-functional team, carefully managing resources, and implementing a robust change management plan, the small organization successfully overcame challenges during ITIL4 adoption. This case study serves as an inspiring example for IT professionals looking to implement ITIL4 in their organizations. It emphasizes the importance of collaboration, resourcefulness, and effective change management strategies to achieve successful ITIL4 adoption even in small organizations with limited resources.

Lessons learned and best practices from real-world examples

In the fast-paced world of IT, keeping up with the latest industry standards and best practices is crucial for success. One such framework that has gained immense popularity over the years is ITIL (Information Technology Infrastructure Library). ITIL provides a comprehensive set of guidelines and practices to efficiently manage IT services within an organization. However, implementing ITIL4 in your organization can be a daunting task without proper guidance. That's where real-world examples come into play, offering valuable lessons learned and best practices to help IT professionals navigate the implementation process smoothly.

Real-world examples provide a unique opportunity to learn from the experiences of others. By studying successful ITIL4 implementations in various organizations, IT professionals can gain insights into the challenges they may encounter and the strategies to overcome them. These examples shed light on the importance of proper planning, stakeholder engagement, and effective communication throughout the implementation journey.

One crucial lesson learned from real-world examples is the significance of gaining buy-in from top management. ITIL4 implementation requires a cultural shift within the organization, and without the support and commitment of senior leaders, the process may face resistance and fail to yield the desired results. Real-world examples demonstrate how successful organizations effectively engaged their leadership, aligning the ITIL4 implementation with the overall business goals and objectives.

Another valuable lesson learned from real-world examples is the importance of starting small and gradually scaling up. Implementing ITIL4 across an entire organization at once can be overwhelming and may lead to confusion and resistance. Real-world examples illustrate how organizations achieved success by piloting ITIL4 practices in one department or service, ensuring that the new processes were well understood and embraced by the team before expanding to other areas.

Additionally, real-world examples highlight the significance of continuous improvement and learning from feedback. ITIL4 implementation is an ongoing journey, and organizations that constantly evaluate and refine their processes based on feedback from users and stakeholders are more likely to achieve long-term success.

By studying real-world examples, IT professionals can gain valuable insights into the practical application of ITIL4 in different organizational contexts. These examples provide a roadmap for success, showcasing the lessons learned and best practices that can guide IT professionals in implementing ITIL4 effectively and efficiently within their organizations. With the right knowledge and understanding, IT professionals can leverage ITIL4 to optimize IT services, enhance customer satisfaction, and drive business growth.

Chapter 12: ITIL4 Training and Certification

Understanding the ITIL4 certification levels and requirements

In today's fast-paced digital landscape, IT professionals are constantly seeking ways to enhance their skills and expertise to meet the ever-evolving demands of the industry. One of the most sought-after certifications in the IT service management domain is ITIL4. Developed by AXELOS, ITIL4 provides a comprehensive framework that enables organizations to align their IT services with their business objectives. This section aims to provide IT professionals with a clear understanding of the various certification levels and requirements associated with ITIL4.

ITIL4 offers a structured approach to IT service management, helping organizations improve their service delivery and customer satisfaction. The certification program is divided into four levels, each representing a different depth of understanding and expertise in ITIL4 concepts and practices.

The first level, ITIL4 Foundation, is an entry-level certification that introduces candidates to the key principles and elements of the ITIL4 framework. It is designed to provide a solid foundation and common language for individuals who are new to ITIL4 or have limited experience in IT service management.

Moving up the certification ladder, the next level is ITIL4 Managing Professional (MP). This level is intended for IT professionals who want to specialize in IT service management and demonstrate their ability to plan, implement, and manage ITIL4 practices in an organization. To attain the ITIL4 MP certification, candidates must complete four modules: ITIL4 Specialist Create, Deliver, and Support; ITIL4 Specialist Drive Stakeholder Value; ITIL4 Specialist High-Velocity IT; and ITIL4 Strategist Direct, Plan, and Improve.

The third level is ITIL4 Strategic Leader (SL), which focuses on the business and strategic aspects of IT service management. This level is suitable for IT professionals who hold leadership roles or aspire to lead IT service management initiatives in their organizations. To achieve the ITIL4 SL certification, candidates must complete two modules: ITIL4 Strategist Direct, Plan, and Improve, and ITIL4 Leader Digital and IT Strategy.

Finally, the highest level is ITIL4 Master, which recognizes individuals who have achieved a deep understanding of ITIL4 and can apply its principles in complex, real-world scenarios. The ITIL4 Master certification requires candidates to demonstrate their ability to analyze and solve complex IT service management problems through a written submission and an interview.

To pursue the ITIL4 certifications, IT professionals must meet certain requirements. For the Foundation level, there are no prerequisites. However, to progress to the higher levels, candidates must have obtained the ITIL4 Foundation certification and fulfill specific experience and education criteria.

In conclusion, the ITIL4 certification program offers a progressive and comprehensive learning journey for IT professionals. By acquiring these certifications, IT professionals can demonstrate their expertise in IT service management and contribute to the successful implementation of ITIL4 practices in their organizations. Whether you are just starting your ITIL4 journey or aiming to reach the pinnacle of IT service management, the ITIL4 certification levels provide a clear roadmap to enhance your skills and boost your career prospects.

Choosing the right ITIL4 training provider

As an IT professional looking to implement ITIL4 in your organization, one of the crucial steps is to choose the right training provider. The success of your ITIL4 implementation depends heavily on the knowledge and skills gained through the training, making it imperative to select a provider that meets your specific needs and requirements. This section will guide you through the process of selecting the ideal ITIL4 training provider for your organization.

When considering potential training providers, there are several factors to take into account. First and foremost, look for a provider that is accredited by AXELOS, the governing body for ITIL. Accreditation ensures that the training content and delivery methods are aligned with the official ITIL4 framework, providing you with the most accurate and up-to-date information.

Another critical aspect to consider is the reputation and experience of the training provider. Look for providers with a proven track record of delivering high-quality ITIL training programs. Check for testimonials, reviews, and case studies from previous clients to gauge their expertise and effectiveness.

It is also important to assess the training delivery options offered by the provider. Consider whether they offer both online and in-person training, as this will allow you to choose the most convenient option for your team. Additionally, evaluate the flexibility of their training schedules to ensure they accommodate your organization's needs.

Furthermore, look for training providers that offer comprehensive course materials and resources. ITIL4 is a complex framework, and having access to well-structured and detailed materials will aid in your understanding and application of ITIL principles. Ask for sample course materials or syllabi to assess their depth and relevance.

Cost is another crucial factor to consider when selecting a training provider. Evaluate the price of their training programs concerning the value they offer. Remember that the cheapest option may not always be the best, as quality and effectiveness should be prioritized over cost alone.

Lastly, consider the post-training support provided by the training provider. Look for providers that offer additional resources such as access to online communities, forums, or expert consultation. These resources will prove invaluable as you implement ITIL4 in your organization and encounter real-world challenges.

Choosing the right ITIL4 training provider is a critical step toward successfully implementing ITIL4 in your organization. By considering factors such as accreditation, reputation, training delivery options, course materials, cost, and post-training support, you can ensure that you select a provider that aligns with your organization's needs and goals. Investing in high-quality ITIL4 training will equip you and your team with the necessary knowledge and skills to drive effective IT service management and deliver value to your organization.

Preparing for the ITIL4 certification exams

In today's rapidly evolving IT landscape, staying updated with the latest industry practices is crucial for IT professionals. The IT Infrastructure Library (ITIL) has long been regarded as the gold standard for IT service management, and the latest iteration, ITIL4, introduces several new concepts and practices. To successfully implement ITIL4 in your organization, it is essential to have a team of certified professionals who possess a deep understanding of the framework. This section provides valuable insights and guidance on preparing for the ITIL4 certification exams, empowering IT professionals like you to become certified ITIL4 practitioners.

The ITIL4 certification exams are designed to evaluate your knowledge and understanding of the ITIL4 framework, its principles, practices, and processes. To ensure success in these exams, a systematic approach to preparation is necessary. Here are some key steps to help you prepare effectively:

1. Understand the ITIL4 Framework: Familiarize yourself with the ITIL4 framework by studying the official ITIL4 publications. Gain a comprehensive understanding of the guiding principles, service value system, and key concepts.

2. Select the Appropriate Certification Level: ITIL4 offers various certification levels, ranging from Foundation to Master. Determine the appropriate level based on your experience, knowledge, and career aspirations.

3. Enroll in a Training Program: Participating in a structured training program led by experienced ITIL4 trainers can significantly enhance your understanding of the framework. Look for accredited training providers who offer comprehensive courses specifically designed for the certification exams.

4. Practice with Sample Exams: To familiarize yourself with the format and types of questions asked in the certification exams, make use of sample exams available in books and online resources. Practice exams will help you identify areas where you need to focus more attention.

5. Collaborate and Share Knowledge: Engage with fellow IT professionals who are also preparing for the ITIL4 exams. Form study groups, attend forums, or join online communities to discuss concepts, share resources, and learn from each other's experiences.

6. Create a Study Plan: Develop a structured study plan that covers all the key topics and allows sufficient time for revision. Break down the syllabus into manageable sections and allocate dedicated study time for each.

7. Review and Revise: Regularly review your notes, textbooks, and online resources to reinforce your understanding of ITIL4 concepts.

Focus on areas that you find challenging and revise them thoroughly.

By following these steps and dedicating time and effort to your preparation, you can increase your chances of successfully passing the ITIL4 certification exams. Becoming a certified ITIL4 practitioner not only enhances your professional credibility but also equips you with the knowledge and skills to effectively implement ITIL4 practices within your organization.

Remember, ITIL4 certification is a continuous journey. Once you obtain your certification, continue to stay updated with the latest developments in the ITIL4 framework through ongoing professional development and participation in ITIL4 community events. Your commitment to lifelong learning will ensure you remain at the forefront of IT service management practices and contribute to the success of your organization's ITIL4 implementation.

Chapter 13: ITIL4 Adoption Challenges and Pitfalls to Avoid

Common challenges faced during ITIL4 implementation

Implementing ITIL4 in your organization can bring about numerous benefits such as improved service quality, increased customer satisfaction, and enhanced efficiency. However, like any significant organizational change, there are common challenges that IT professionals may encounter during the ITIL4 implementation process. This section aims to address these challenges and provide insights on how to overcome them successfully.

One of the primary challenges faced during ITIL4 implementation is resistance to change. Employees may be accustomed to the existing processes and may resist adopting new practices. Overcoming this challenge requires effective change management strategies, including clear communication about the benefits of ITIL4, engaging employees in the decision-making process, and providing comprehensive training on the new processes and tools.

Another common challenge is the lack of leadership support and commitment. ITIL4 implementation requires strong leadership to drive the change and ensure its successful adoption throughout the organization. To address this challenge, IT professionals must work towards gaining executive buy-in and support, emphasizing the potential positive impact on business outcomes, and aligning ITIL4 implementation with the organization's strategic objectives.

Integration with existing systems and processes is also a significant challenge. Organizations often have complex IT infrastructures and processes in place, which may not align with the ITIL4 framework. IT professionals need to carefully assess the existing systems, identify gaps or redundancies, and plan for a smooth integration of ITIL4 practices. This may involve customization or modification of existing processes, tools, and technologies.

Resource constraints, such as limited budget and staffing, can also hinder ITIL4 implementation. It is crucial for IT professionals to demonstrate the return on investment and the long-term benefits of adopting ITIL4 practices to secure the necessary resources. Prioritizing initiatives, leveraging automation and technology, and seeking external support or partnerships can also help overcome resource challenges.

Lastly, measuring and demonstrating the value of ITIL4 can be a challenge. IT professionals should define key performance indicators (KPIs) aligned with organizational goals and regularly monitor and report on the progress and impact of ITIL4 implementation. This will help build credibility and support for the initiative.

In conclusion, while implementing ITIL4 in your organization can be challenging, being aware of the common obstacles and having strategies to overcome them will greatly increase the chances of success. By addressing resistance to change, gaining leadership support, integrating with existing systems, managing resource constraints, and measuring value, IT professionals can successfully implement ITIL4 and reap the benefits of improved IT service management.

Strategies for overcoming resistance to change

Introduction:

Implementing ITIL4 in an organization is a transformative process that can lead to improved efficiency, enhanced service delivery, and increased customer satisfaction. However, change is often met with resistance, and it is essential for IT professionals to be prepared to address and overcome this resistance. In this section, we will explore effective strategies for managing resistance to change during the ITIL4 implementation journey.

1. Communicate the Vision:

One of the most crucial strategies for overcoming resistance to change is effective communication. Clearly articulate the vision and benefits of ITIL4 implementation to the entire organization. Highlight how it aligns with the business objectives and addresses pain points. Regularly communicate updates, success stories, and milestones to keep everyone engaged and motivated.

2. Create a Sense of Urgency:

Resistance to change can often be attributed to a lack of understanding about the need for change. Create a sense of urgency by highlighting the potential risks and missed opportunities if the organization fails to adopt ITIL4. Showcase industry trends and competitors who have successfully implemented ITIL4 to emphasize the importance of staying ahead.

3. Involve Stakeholders:

Engaging stakeholders from different levels and departments is vital for successful change management. Involve key individuals in the decision-making process to gain their buy-in and address their concerns. Their involvement will not only provide valuable insights but also create a sense of ownership and accountability.

4. Provide Training and Support:

Resistance to change can often stem from a fear of the unknown. Provide comprehensive training programs to equip employees with the necessary skills and knowledge to embrace ITIL4. Offer ongoing support through workshops, coaching, and mentoring to help employees navigate the implementation process and address any challenges they may face.

5. Celebrate Quick Wins:

Celebrate and communicate quick wins achieved through the ITIL4 implementation process. Highlight success stories and recognize individuals or teams for their contributions. This will not only boost morale but also demonstrate the positive impact of change, encouraging others to embrace it.

6. Address Resistance Proactively:

Proactively identify and address resistance to change. Listen to employees' concerns and provide clarity and guidance. Understand that resistance may arise due to fear, lack of trust, or misinformation. Address these issues promptly and transparently to build a positive environment for change.

Conclusion:

Implementing ITIL4 in your organization requires effective change management strategies to overcome resistance. By communicating the vision, creating a sense of urgency, involving stakeholders, providing training and support, celebrating quick wins, and addressing resistance proactively, IT professionals can navigate the journey successfully. Embracing these strategies will not only ensure a smoother transition but also create a culture of continuous improvement and growth within the organization.

Avoiding common pitfalls and ensuring successful ITIL4 adoption

As an IT professional looking to implement ITIL4 in your organization, it is crucial to be aware of the common pitfalls that can hinder a smooth transition and successful adoption. With proper planning and careful execution, you can navigate these challenges and position your organization for long-term success. This section provides valuable insights and practical advice to help you avoid these pitfalls and ensure a successful ITIL4 adoption journey.

One common pitfall is the lack of clear understanding and communication about the purpose and benefits of ITIL4. It is essential to educate stakeholders, including senior management and end-users, about the positive impact that ITIL4 principles and practices can have on the organization's efficiency, productivity, and customer satisfaction. By clearly articulating the value proposition of ITIL4, you can gain buy-in and support from key decision-makers and ensure a smoother adoption process.

Another pitfall to avoid is attempting to implement ITIL4 in isolation, without considering the organization's existing processes and culture. It is important to conduct a thorough assessment of the current state of IT service management within your organization, identifying areas of strength and weakness. By aligning ITIL4 practices with existing processes and addressing any gaps or inconsistencies, you can ensure a more seamless integration and minimize disruption to daily operations.

Resistance to change is another common obstacle that can impede successful ITIL4 adoption. It is crucial to anticipate and address resistance by involving key stakeholders early on and fostering a culture of collaboration and continuous improvement. By involving employees at all levels and providing them with the necessary training and support, you can mitigate resistance and create a sense of ownership and engagement in the ITIL4 adoption process.

Furthermore, inadequate planning and unrealistic expectations can hinder the success of ITIL4 adoption. It is important to establish a clear roadmap and set realistic goals and timelines for implementation. By breaking down the adoption process into manageable phases and regularly monitoring progress, you can ensure that your organization stays on track and achieves its desired outcomes.

In conclusion, successful ITIL4 adoption requires careful planning, effective communication, and a proactive approach to addressing potential pitfalls. By avoiding common mistakes and ensuring a holistic approach to implementation, you can position your organization for long-term success in improving IT service management. This section serves as a valuable guide for IT professionals, providing them with the necessary knowledge and insights to navigate the challenges and achieve a successful ITIL4 adoption journey.

Chapter 14: Building a Culture of Continuous Improvement

Fostering a culture of continuous improvement within your organization

In today's fast-paced and ever-evolving technological landscape, it is crucial for IT professionals to embrace a culture of continuous improvement within their organizations. This section aims to provide practical guidance on how to implement ITIL4 and cultivate a mindset that values innovation, efficiency, and growth.

Continuous improvement is not just a buzzword; it is a fundamental principle that drives organizations towards success. By continuously seeking ways to enhance processes, procedures, and services, IT professionals can stay ahead of the curve and deliver exceptional value to their customers.

The first step in fostering a culture of continuous improvement is to establish a clear vision and set of objectives. ITIL4 provides a comprehensive framework that can guide professionals in aligning their goals with the organization's overall strategy. By understanding the organization's priorities, IT professionals can identify areas that require improvement and develop a roadmap for achieving their objectives.

Communication and collaboration are essential components of a culture of continuous improvement. IT professionals should engage with stakeholders, both internal and external, to gather feedback and insights. By actively listening to the needs and expectations of customers, IT professionals can identify gaps in their services and implement necessary changes.

Regularly conducting assessments and audits is another crucial aspect of fostering continuous improvement. By regularly evaluating the performance of processes, procedures, and services, IT professionals can identify areas of improvement and implement corrective actions. ITIL4 provides a range of tools and techniques, such as service reviews and maturity assessments, that can aid in this process.

Training and development are vital to cultivating a culture of continuous improvement. IT professionals should be provided with opportunities to enhance their skills and knowledge, enabling them to contribute effectively to the organization's improvement initiatives. By investing in professional development, organizations can build a team that is equipped to tackle challenges and drive innovation.

Lastly, the culture of continuous improvement should be supported by a robust feedback mechanism. IT professionals should encourage and appreciate ideas and suggestions from all levels within the organization. By recognizing and rewarding innovation, organizations can motivate their employees to actively participate in improvement initiatives.

In conclusion, fostering a culture of continuous improvement within an organization is a journey that requires commitment, collaboration, and a willingness to embrace change. By implementing ITIL4 and following the practical guidance provided in this section, IT professionals can drive innovation, enhance efficiency, and deliver exceptional value to their customers.

Engaging and empowering IT professionals for ongoing ITIL4 success

In today's rapidly evolving technological landscape, the implementation of ITIL4 has become imperative for organizations striving to enhance their IT service management practices. However, successful implementation of ITIL4 goes beyond the adoption of processes and tools; it requires the engagement and empowerment of IT professionals, who play a critical role in driving the transformation.

Engagement is the key to unlocking the potential of IT professionals and fostering a culture of continuous improvement. It involves creating a shared vision and aligning individual goals with organizational objectives. By engaging IT professionals, organizations can tap into their expertise, ideas, and creativity to drive the successful implementation of ITIL4.

One way to engage IT professionals is by involving them in the decision-making process. Seek their input and feedback when designing and implementing ITIL4 processes. This not only demonstrates trust and respect for their expertise but also ensures that the solutions and improvements are tailored to the specific needs of the organization. Engaging IT professionals in this way fosters a sense of ownership, accountability, and commitment to the success of ITIL4.

Empowering IT professionals is equally crucial for ongoing ITIL4 success. Empowerment involves providing the necessary tools, resources,
and authority to make decisions and take action. It encourages IT
professionals to take ownership of their work, be proactive in problem-
solving, and continuously seek opportunities for self-improvement.

To empower IT professionals, organizations should invest in training
and development programs that enable them to acquire the skills
and knowledge required to implement ITIL4 effectively. This not
only enhances their capabilities but also boosts their confidence and
motivation to drive positive change. Additionally, providing access to
relevant documentation, knowledge bases, and collaboration platforms
empowers IT professionals to access information and collaborate with
their peers, enabling them to make informed decisions and drive
continuous improvement.

Moreover, recognizing and rewarding the contributions of IT professionals is essential for sustaining their engagement and empowering
them for ongoing ITIL4 success. Acknowledge their achievements,
whether big or small, and celebrate their successes. This creates a positive work environment that fosters motivation, encourages innovation,
and reinforces the value of their efforts in implementing ITIL4.

In conclusion, engaging and empowering IT professionals is vital for
the ongoing success of ITIL4 implementation. By involving them
in decision-making, providing them with the necessary tools and
resources, and recognizing their contributions, organizations can
harness the expertise, creativity, and motivation of IT professionals
to drive continuous improvement and achieve the desired outcomes

of ITIL4 implementation. Together, IT professionals can spearhead the transformation and pave the way for organizational success in the digital age.

Sustaining and evolving your ITIL4 practices over time

In today's rapidly changing technological landscape, it is crucial for organizations to constantly evolve and adapt their IT service management practices. Implementing ITIL4 is a step in the right direction, but it is equally important to sustain and evolve these practices over time to ensure continued success and alignment with business goals. This section will provide valuable insights and guidance on how IT professionals can sustain and evolve their ITIL4 practices in their organizations.

1. Continuous Improvement: ITIL4 promotes a culture of continuous improvement, where organizations are encouraged to regularly assess their processes, identify areas for improvement, and implement changes accordingly. IT professionals should embrace this mindset and actively seek feedback from stakeholders to identify opportunities for refinement and enhancement.

2. Training and Development: As ITIL4 evolves, it is vital for IT professionals to stay updated with the latest best practices and frameworks. Organizations must invest in training and development programs to ensure that their IT professionals have the necessary knowledge and skills to effectively implement and sustain ITIL4 practices. This can include attending ITIL4 certification courses, participating in workshops, and staying connected with the IT service management community.

3. Change Management: ITIL4 recognizes the importance of effective change management in ensuring smooth transitions and minimizing disruptions. IT professionals should establish robust change management processes and systems to manage and control changes to IT services, infrastructure, and applications. This includes documenting and communicating change requests, assessing potential impacts, and obtaining necessary approvals.

4. Collaboration and Communication: Successful implementation and sustainability of ITIL4 practices require effective collaboration and communication across different teams and departments. IT professionals should foster a culture of open communication, promote cross-functional collaboration, and establish clear channels for sharing information and knowledge. This can be achieved through regular meetings, workshops, and the use of collaboration tools and platforms.

5. Monitoring and Measurement: To ensure the effectiveness of ITIL4 practices, IT professionals should establish key performance indicators (KPIs) and regularly monitor and measure their progress. This includes tracking metrics such as incident resolution times, service availability, customer satisfaction, and the effectiveness of problem management processes. By analyzing these metrics, IT professionals can identify areas for improvement and make data-driven decisions.

In conclusion, sustaining and evolving ITIL4 practices over time is essential for organizations to stay ahead in the rapidly changing IT landscape. By embracing a culture of continuous improvement, investing in training and development, implementing robust change management processes, fostering collaboration and communication, and monitoring and measuring progress, IT professionals can ensure the long-term success and alignment of ITIL4 practices with business goals.

Chapter 15: Conclusion

Recap of key concepts and takeaways

In this section, we will recap the key concepts and takeaways from our journey through "ITIL4 in Action: A Step-by-Step Guide for IT Professionals". As IT professionals looking to implement ITIL4 in your organization, it is crucial to have a clear understanding of the foundational principles and key takeaways to ensure successful implementation and adoption.

One of the fundamental concepts of ITIL4 is the service value system (SVS). The SVS provides a holistic approach to delivering value to customers through a combination of guiding principles, governance, and practices. Understanding the SVS and its components, such as the guiding principles and governance, is essential for aligning IT services with business objectives and maximizing value delivery.

Another key concept is the four dimensions of service management. These dimensions - organizations and people, information and technology, partners and suppliers, and value streams and processes - provide a comprehensive view of the various aspects that need to be considered when designing, delivering, and improving IT services. By addressing these dimensions, you can ensure that your organization's IT services are well-rounded and meet the needs of both the business and customers.

Throughout the book, we have also emphasized the importance of continual improvement. ITIL4 encourages organizations to adopt a culture of continuous learning and improvement to enhance their services and stay ahead in a rapidly evolving IT landscape. By leveraging practices such as the continual improvement model and the ITIL4 practices, you can proactively identify areas for improvement and implement changes that deliver tangible benefits.

Furthermore, the book has laid out a step-by-step approach to implementing ITIL4 in your organization. From assessing your current state to defining your desired future state, from building a strong foundation to continuously improving your services, each step has been carefully explained.

In conclusion, as IT professionals looking to implement ITIL4 in your organization, it is crucial to grasp the key concepts and takeaways discussed in this book. By understanding the service value system, the four dimensions of service management, and the importance of continual improvement, you can effectively align IT services with business objectives and deliver maximum value to your customers. The step-by-step implementation approach presented in this book will guide you in designing, implementing, and continuously improving your IT services, ensuring long-term success for your organization.

Final thoughts on implementing ITIL4 in your organization

As IT professionals, you understand the importance of implementing best practices in your organization to enhance service delivery and drive business success. In today's fast-paced and technology-driven world, ITIL4 has emerged as a comprehensive framework that enables organizations to align their IT services with business needs. Throughout this book, we have explored the step-by-step process of implementing ITIL4, and in this final section, we will provide some key thoughts and insights to help you successfully implement ITIL4 in your organization.

First and foremost, it is crucial to understand that implementing ITIL4 is not a one-time project, but an ongoing journey. The framework is designed to be flexible and adaptable to changing business require- ments, ensuring that your organization can continuously improve its IT service management practices. Embracing a mindset of continuous improvement will be essential to fully leverage the benefits of ITIL4.

Another important aspect to consider is the need for strong leadership and commitment from the top management. Implementing ITIL4 requires a cultural shift within the organization, and this can only be achieved if the leadership is fully supportive and actively involved in the process. Leaders should communicate the vision, set clear expectations, and provide the necessary resources and support to make the implementation a success.

Furthermore, it is crucial to involve all relevant stakeholders throughout the implementation process. This includes IT staff, business users, and customers. By bringing together different perspectives and experiences, you can ensure that the implemented ITIL4 practices truly align with the needs of your organization.

Additionally, it is important to remember that ITIL4 is not a set of rigid rules, but a framework that can be tailored to suit your organization's unique requirements. While it provides best practices and guidelines, it is essential to adapt and customize the framework to fit your organization's specific context. This will ensure that the implementation is meaningful and relevant to your business.

Lastly, monitoring and measuring the effectiveness of your ITIL4 implementation is crucial. Regularly assess the performance of your IT services, identify areas for improvement, and make necessary adjustments. By doing so, you can continuously enhance the value and efficiency of your IT services, ultimately contributing to the overall success of your organization.

In conclusion, implementing ITIL4 in your organization is a journey that requires commitment, leadership, and a continuous improvement mindset. By embracing the framework and tailoring it to your organization's needs, you can enhance service delivery, align IT with business objectives, and drive long-term success. Remember, ITIL4 is not a destination, but a tool that empowers organizations to adapt, evolve, and excel in the ever-changing IT landscape.

Looking ahead: Future trends and developments in IT service management and ITIL4

As an IT professional, staying ahead of the curve is essential to ensure the success of your organization's IT service management practices. In this section, we will explore the future trends and developments in IT service management and how ITIL4 can help you implement them in your organization.

The digital age is transforming the way we do business, and IT service management is no exception. With the rapid advancement of technology, IT professionals need to adapt and embrace emerging trends to deliver efficient and effective IT services. Here are some key trends to look out for:

1. Automation and AI: The rise of automation and artificial intelligence is revolutionizing IT service management. Intelligent automation can help streamline processes, reduce human errors, and improve service quality. ITIL4 guides how to leverage automation and AI to enhance service delivery.

2. Agile and DevOps: Agile methodologies and DevOps practices are becoming increasingly popular in IT service management. These approaches emphasize collaboration, flexibility, and continuous improvement. ITIL4 incorporates agile and DevOps principles, helping IT professionals adopt a more agile mindset and improve the speed and quality of service delivery.

3. Cloud Computing: Cloud computing has revolutionized the way IT services are delivered. It offers scalability, flexibility, and cost-effectiveness. ITIL4 guides how to effectively manage and govern cloud services, ensuring optimal performance and security.

4. Customer Experience: Customer experience is a top priority for organizations. IT service management should focus on delivering exceptional customer service and meeting user expectations. ITIL4 emphasizes the importance of customer-centricity and guides how to design and deliver services that align with customer needs.

5. Cybersecurity: With the increasing frequency and complexity of cyber threats, cybersecurity is a critical concern for IT professionals. ITIL4 addresses cybersecurity considerations and guides how to effectively manage and mitigate risks.

Implementing ITIL4 in your organization can help you navigate these future trends and developments. ITIL4 provides a comprehensive framework and best practices for IT service management, enabling you to align IT services with business objectives, improve service quality, and drive continuous improvement.

By embracing these future trends and leveraging the capabilities of ITIL4, IT professionals can position themselves as strategic partners within their organizations. They can drive innovation, enhance service delivery, and contribute to the overall success of the business.

In conclusion, the future of IT service management is bright and exciting. By staying informed about the latest trends and developments and adopting ITIL4, IT professionals can ensure their organizations are well-prepared to thrive in the digital age. So, take the lead, embrace change, and embark on a journey of continuous improvement with ITIL4.

About the Author

Edgardo Fernandez Climent, an accomplished IT professional with over two decades of experience, has left an indelible mark in the realms of infrastructure, networks, and cybersecurity. After graduating with honors in Computer Information Systems, Edgardo pursued an MBA and a Master's in Management Information Systems degree. He holds several industry certifications such as PMP, ITIL4, and Security+ among others.

Throughout his career, Edgardo's commitment to staying abreast of emerging technologies and industry trends remained unwavering. His leadership in steering organizations through complex technological landscapes and safeguarding them against cyber threats has become a testament to his expertise and foresight.

Not just a technical virtuoso, Edgardo also earned a reputation for mentoring and inspiring the next generation of IT professionals. His dedication to knowledge-sharing and fostering a collaborative work environment has left a lasting impact on the teams he led.

Today, as a sought-after consultant in the IT industry, Edgardo continues to shape the technological landscape, driving innovation and fortifying organizations against the ever-evolving challenges of the digital era. His journey stands as a testament to the transformative power of experience, expertise, and a relentless pursuit of excellence in the dynamic field of information technology.

www.ingramcontent.com/pod-product-compliance
Lightning Source LLC
La Vergne TN
LVHW051344050326
832903LV00031B/3723